Drama Decoded

TRADITION MEETS SCIENCE

SHEETAL AGRAWAL

BLUEROSE PUBLISHERS
India | U.K.

Copyright © Sheetal Agrawal 2025

All rights reserved by author. No part of this publication may be reproduced, stored in a retrieval system or transmitted in any form or by any means, electronic, mechanical, photocopying, recording or otherwise, without the prior permission of the author. Although every precaution has been taken to verify the accuracy of the information contained herein, the publisher assumes no responsibility for any errors or omissions. No liability is assumed for damages that may result from the use of information contained within.

BlueRose Publishers takes no responsibility for any damages, losses, or liabilities that may arise from the use or misuse of the information, products, or services provided in this publication.

For permissions requests or inquiries regarding this publication, please contact:

BLUEROSE PUBLISHERS
www.BlueRoseONE.com
info@bluerosepublishers.com
+91 8882 898 898
+4407342408967

ISBN: 978-93-6783-238-7

Cover Design: Aman Sharma
Typesetting: Pooja Sharma

First Edition: February 2025

Introduction by the Author

As a child spirituality and religion were never a part of my consciousness I grew up in a world where practical concerns took centre-stage, and the idea of divine forces or deep spiritual insights felt distant and irrelevant my life was anchored in the tangible school career ambitions friendships and the daily routines that most of us follow. I never really gave much thought to the deeper aspects of life much less the spiritual or religious traditions that was so prevalent in my Hindu household. The rituals for my prayers and customs that my family followed seemed like things to do out of routine rather than with any profound purpose. but life has a way of leading us down unexpected path and over time my perception of life began to change in ways I could never have anticipated. The journey I'm about to share with you isn't one that began with a sudden epiphany or a desire to become spiritually enlightened. It was a gradual process, one shipped by experiences, challenges and enough transformations. Life as it often does through challenges my way- challenges that forced me to reflect on my existence, my beliefs, on my connection to something greater than myself. This is when I started questioning the nature of life, the purpose of human existence, and the meaning behind the rituals and traditions of my culture.

It was only when life took a different turn when things that once seemed certain became uncertain- that I began to feel a deep yearning for something more. I had reached a point where the material world no longer satisfied my inner longing. There was a sense of emptiness that nothing could fill. Despite achieving professional success and personal milestones, I found myself struggling with an internal void that no achievement seemed to solve. This led me to seek answers in a way I never had before.

The first step in my spiritual journey was simple curiosity. I began asking questions- questions I had never dared to ask earlier. Why do we pray? Why do we perform certain rituals? What is the significance of many festivals and customs we observe in Hindu society? What is the meaning behind the sacred text and scriptures? I realise that many of these practises were not just cultural or familial obligations, but they had deep spiritual roots and profound significance. Slowly, I began to explore the rich traditions of Hinduism not from an intellectual standpoint, but from a heart full of questions and spirit ready to listen.

As I delved deeper into the teachings of ancient sages and spiritual leaders, i discovered that Hinduism is not merely a religion, but a way of life- a philosophy that teaches us to live harmoniously with the world around us, to understand our true nature, and to see unity with the divine food stop I began to see the beauty and wisdom in the rituals I had once dismissed flint stop the offerings of flowers and fruits In prayer we're not just symbolic gestures but deep expression of gratitude and devotion. The chance and mantras were not just words, they were tools for focusing the mind, aligning with the higher self on tapping into the universal energy that surrounds us.

In this book, I want to take you through my personal transformation- from a non-spiritual sceptical person to someone who finds solace, peace an understanding in the vast and timeless traditions of Hinduism. Want to share with you the lessons I have learned, the wisdom I have encountered, and the beauty that i have found in these traditions. More than just describing rituals or customs comma i hope to offer insights into, i hope to offer insights into the deeper meanings Behind them, showing how they can be applied in our everyday lives to bring us closer to spiritual fulfilment an inner peace.

My journey into spirituality was not a linear path. There were times of doubt, confusion and frustration, but it was through these struggles that I grew the most. Each step brought me closer to understanding my own true nature and the interconnectedness of all beings. I came to realise that spirituality isn't just about rituals and beliefs, it's about a deeper connection to the universe and the divine, about finding meaning in life's simplest moments, and about transforming oneself from the inside out.

As I look back on my journey, i see how each experience, whether painful or joyful, was a stepping stone that brought me closer to this new understanding. I have learned to see life not as a series of random events, but as a divine play where each moment carries its own significance would stop through the teachings of the great sages and through my own reflections, i have come to appreciate the profound depth of hindu traditions and their timeless wisdom please stop

This book is not just a narrative of my spiritual journey, it is a call to anyone who feels lost, disconnected all uncertain about the purpose of life. If you have ever wondered about the deeper meaning behind the customs you see in Hindu society, or if you have ever felt the need for something more than what the material world can offer, then this book is for you. My story is not unique, it reflects the universal search for meaning and truth and connection.

I hope that through the lessons I share, you too will begin to see the profound wisdom in the traditions that have been passed down through generations please stop these traditions are not just relics of the past- they are living, breathing practises that can guide us in our everyday lives, bringing us closer to the divine and helping us lead more peaceful, fulfilled lives.

As you turn the pages of the book, i invite you to join me on this journey- one that continues to unfold, bringing you insights an understanding at every turn. Let us explore together the deeper meaning of life and the divine, as found in the spiritual traditions of Hinduism.

As you reach the end of this introduction, i want to take a moment to express my heartfelt gratitude to you, the reader, for choosing this book. In a world full of distractions and choices, the fact that you have picked up these pages means that there is a part of you seeking answers, seeking understanding, or perhaps simply curious about the deeper meaning of life and the traditions that surround us. May this book serve as a gentle reminder that spirituality is not something distant, but something that resides within us, waiting to be discovered. Thank you for allowing me to share my story and thoughts with you.

Contents

Chapter 1: The Importance and Story Behind Ganesh Vandana.. 1

Chapter 2: The Timeless Devotion to Lord Hanuman 6

Chapter 3: The Story Behind Jyotirlingas and their Importance.. 18

Chapter 4 : The Sacred Shakti Peeths and the Divine Feminine Power 25

Chapter 5 : The Toe Ring—A Symbol of Tradition and its Hidden Power 29

Chapter 6: Piercings – The Painful Yet Meaningful Journey.. 33

Chapter 7: The Unseen Power of Tradition – Understanding the Restrictions During My Periods 36

Chapter 8: The Dilemma of Sindoor – Unraveling the Mystery Behind Tradition 40

Chapter 9: The Significance of Going Barefoot in a Temple ... 44

Chapter 10: The Significance of the Mangalsutra 47

Chapter 11: The Science Behind Wearing Gold in the Upper Part of the Body and Silver in the Lower Part of the Body 54

Chapter 12: The Science Behind Women Wearing Raksha Sutra in Left Hand and Men in Right Hand 59

Chapter 13: The Relation Between the Moon Cycle and Menstruation 64

Chapter 14: The Science Behind Wearing a Copper Ring 69

Chapter 15: Water and Energy: The Transformative Influence of External Forces on Molecular Structure 73

Chapter 16: The Science Behind Sleeping Direction 78

Chapter 17: The Science Behind Janayu Sanskar 82

Chapter 18: The Significance of Ritu Kala Samskara 86

Chapter 19: The Celebration of Menstruation at Kamakhya Devi Temple 91

Chapter 20: The Meaning and Importance of the 16 Sanskaras 96

Chapter 21: The Science Behind Trikal Sadhana 101

Chapter 22: The Science Behind Chanting AUM 106

Chapter 23: The Importance of Kapoor Aarti at the End of Puja 111

Chapter 24: Why Do We Sprinkle Water Around Food Before Eating? 116

Chapter 25: Meaning and Significance of the Gayatri Mantra 120

Chapter 26: Science Behind Offering Coconut in Temple 125

Chapter 27: Meaning and Importance of Swastik 129

Chapter 28: Meaning and Importance of Rituals After Death 133

Chapter 29: The Significance of Eclipse in Hindu Tradition 138

Chapter 30: Significance of Jal Deepak 143

Chapter 31: Science Behind Surya Namaskar 148

Chapter 32: How Does the Digestive System Function as Per Sunrise and Sunset 153

Chapter	Title	Page
Chapter 33:	Science Behind Drinking Water Energized in Different Coloured Bottles	158
Chapter 34:	Mitahar (Balanced Diet)	163
Chapter 35:	Science of Touching Feet to Take Blessings	169
Chapter 36:	Anulom Vilom and Nadi Shodhan	174
Chapter 37:	Tratak Kriya	179
Chapter 38:	The Meaning and Way of Reading the Bhagavad Gita	185
Chapter 39:	Solving Day-to-Day Life Questions Through the Bhagavad Gita	190
Chapter 40:	Guru Diksha	203
Chapter 41:	Do Haircuts According to Moon Phase Help in Hair Growth	207
Chapter 42:	Pradakshina: Why Do We Go Clockwise Around Temples	210
Chapter 43:	What Happens If You Don't Eat for a Full Day? (24-hour fast)	213
Chapter 44:	Kumbh Mela, Explained: Its Mythology, History, Astrology, and Why Millions Flock to It	218
Chapter 45:	Rangoli, A Colourful Science of Symmetry	221
Conclusion		224

Chapter 1:
The Importance and Story Behind Ganesh Vandana

In Hindu culture, the beginning of any new venture- whether it's starting a new job, beginning a new project, purchasing a new vehicle, or even initiating a journey- is often marked by the ritual of Ganesh Vandana- prayer to Lord Ganesha. This tradition is not just a matter of following custom but holds deep spiritual significance. Lord Ganesha, the elephant headed diety, is revered as a removal of obstacles and the God of new beginning. In this chapter, we will explore why Ganesh Vandana is so integral to hindu tradition and the story behind this powerful and beloved ritual.

Lord Ganesha: the remover of obstacles

Before diving into the specifics of Ganesh Vandana, it is important to understand who Lord Ganesha is and why he holds such a central role in the spiritual and cultural fabric of Hinduism. Ganesha is the son of Lord Shiva and goddess Parvati, two of the most powerful dieites in Hinduism. While ganesha is worshipped in various forms across the Hindu world, his symbolic remains universal.

The most widely recognised aspect off Lord Ganesha is his role as the remover of obstacle- Vighnahara. Ganisha is believed to have the divine power to clear both physical and mental hurdles that may come in the way of progress and success. He is also the god of wisdom, knowledge, and intellect, and is revered for his ability to bring prosperity unsuccess in any endeavour. His form, which combines the body of a human under head off an elephant, symbolises the balance between the earthly and the divine, the intellect under strength, the material and the spiritual.

when we offer Ganesh vandana before starting something new, we are acknowledging that, despite our best efforts and planning, there are countless unseen forces add play in the universe. By invoking Lord Ganesha, we are seeking his blessings to ensure that our endeavour will proceed smoothly, without unnecessary obstacle. In many ways, ganesh Vandana represents our trust in the divine forces on the belief that with their guidance we can overcome challenges and find success.

The story behind Ganesh vandana

The practise of invoking Lord Ganesha before starting any new work has its roots in ancient Hindu mythology. One of the most popular stories about the birth of Ganesha offers an insight into why we begin every new venture with his blessing.

According to one version of the myth, goddess Parvathi, the consort of Lord Shiva, was preparing for a bath and wanted to have someone guard near her door. She created a young boy out of the turmeric paste she used for her bath and gave him life. This boy whom she named Ganesha was instructed to stand guard and not allow anyone to enter while she bothered.

When Lord shiva returned, unaware of the boy, Ganesha refused to let him enter, following his mother's instruction. Angered by this, shiva attempted to force his way past Ganesha. When Ganesha persisted in his refusal, lord shiva, in a fit of rage, beheaded the young boy.

When Parvathi learned of the tragedy, she was devastated and demanded that she was restored her son to life. To appease her, lord shiva ordered his followers to bring back the head of the first living creature they found. They came back with the head of an elephant, which Shiva attached to Ganesh's body, bringing him back to life.

Since that day, Lord Ganesha has been depicted with the head of an elephant, and his image has been seen as a powerful symbol of strength wisdom and new beginnings. The elephant herd represents the overcoming of challenges with grace and wisdom, while the large yours symbolise the importance of listening carefully and the small mouth signifies the virtue of speaking less and thinking more.

The Mythological Roots

The tradition of Ganesh Vandana finds its origins in ancient Hindu scriptures, particularly in the Puranas. Among the many stories, one stands out vividly. When Sage Vyasa decided to compose the monumental epic Mahabharata, he chose Lord Ganesha as his scribe. The story goes that Ganesha agreed to write on the condition that Vyasa would dictate without pause. To this, Vyasa cleverly added that Ganesha must understand every word before writing it down. This mutual understanding created a synergy that resulted in one of the greatest literary works in history. Thus, Ganesha became synonymous with intellectual clarity and the ability to overcome hurdles—qualities essential for any new beginning.

The Ritual

Ganesh Vandana is more than a prayer; it is a ritual steeped in reverence and intention. Traditionally, it begins with the chanting of mantras such as "Om Gan Ganapataye Namah," which invoke his divine presence. Offerings of modaks, durva grass, and red flowers are made, each carrying a specific significance. Modaks symbolize spiritual knowledge, durva grass denotes humility, and red flowers represent purity and energy. These offerings, combined with the vibrations of the chants, create an atmosphere of positivity and focus.

Contemporary Significance

In modern times, the practice of Ganesh Vandana transcends religious boundaries and has become a cultural cornerstone. It is performed at inaugurations, academic ceremonies, artistic performances, and even corporate events. The universality of this practice lies in its essence: the human need for assurance and hope when stepping into the unknown.

For instance, in the world of performing arts, dancers and musicians often begin their recital with Ganesh Vandana to seek divine blessings and calm their minds. Similarly, entrepreneurs inaugurating a new business invoke Ganesha's blessings to ensure prosperity and stability. These practices underline the belief that divine grace, combined with human effort, leads to fulfillment.

There are several sources that prove the existence of Lord Ganesha, including:

Archaeological evidence

The first terracotta images of Ganesha were found in the 1st century CE in Ter, Pal, Verrapuram, and Chandraketugarh. Some scholars believe that an elephant-headed figure on Indo-Greek coins from the 1st century BCE may be "incipient Ganesha".

Literary references

The earliest literary reference to Ganesha in Jainism is in Abhidhāna chintāmani of Hemachandra, which dates to the third quarter of the 12th century CE.

Sculptures

There are sculptures of Ganesha in many places, including Central America, Persia, Iran, Afghanistan, China, Japan, Thailand, Cambodia, and many other South-East Asian islands.

Manuscripts and excavations

Excavations and manuscripts from Central America prove that Ganesha was worshipped in the Aztec culture.

Puranas

Stories about the birth of Ganesha are found in the later Puranas, composed from about 600 CE onwards.

Conclusion

Ganesh Vandana is a celebration of beginnings, a ritual that bridges the divine and the mundane. By invoking Lord Ganesha, individuals align themselves with values of wisdom, patience, and perseverance, setting the stage for success. In a world where challenges are inevitable, the tradition of seeking the blessings of the Vighnaharta remains a beacon of hope and resilience.

Chapter 2:
The Timeless Devotion to Lord Hanuman

My journey into the world of Lord Hanuman began when I stumbled upon a book titled *Immortal Talks*. It wasn't just a literary experience; it was an awakening. The book painted vivid portraits of Hanuman as a divine being who transcends time, space, and human limitations. His immortality is not merely a mythological concept; it's a testament to his unwavering devotion, selflessness, and spiritual prowess. This chapter delves into the story behind Lord Hanuman's immortality and unpacks the powerful verses of the Hanuman Chalisa, a devotional hymn that holds profound strength and significance.

The Story of Immortality

Lord Hanuman's immortality, or *amaratva*, is deeply rooted in Hindu mythology. According to the Ramayana, Hanuman's unparalleled devotion to Lord Rama earned him blessings of eternal life and undying relevance. It is said that after the great war in Lanka, when Lord Rama's earthly journey was complete, Hanuman chose to remain on Earth to continue serving humanity and spreading Rama's message.

One popular story highlights a boon given to Hanuman by Lord Shiva and other celestial beings, granting him invincibility and the ability to exist as long as the name of Lord Rama is chanted in the world. This eternal connection to devotion and service underscores why Hanuman is revered as the ultimate devotee and an indomitable force.

Unveiling the Hanuman Chalisa

CHOPAI

Shree Guru Charan Saroj Raj, Nij Man Mukar Sudhari, Barnau Raghuvar Bimal Jasu, Jo dayaku Phal Chari
With the dust of Guru's Lotus feet, I clean the mirror of my mind and then narrate the sacred glory of Sri Ram Chandra, The Supereme among the Raghu dynasty. The giver of the four attainments of life.
Budhi heen Tanu Janike, Sumirow, Pavan Kumar, Bal Buddhi Vidya Dehu Mohi, Harahu Kalesh Bikaar
Knowing myself to be ignorent, I urge you, O Hanuman, The son of Pavan! O Lord! kindly Bestow on me strength, wisdom and knowledge, removing all my miseries and blemishes.
Jai Hanuman Gyan Guna Sagar, Jai Kipis Tihun Lok Ujgaar
Victory of Thee, O Hanuman, Ocean of wisdom and virtue, victory to the Lord of monkeys who is well known in all the three worlds
Ramdoot Atulit Bal Dhamaa, Anjani Putra Pavansut naamaa.
You, the Divine messenger of Ram and repository of immeasurable strength, are also known as Anjaniputra and known as the son of the wind - Pavanputra.
Mahebeer Bikram Bajrangi, Kumati Nivaar Sumati Ke Sangi.
Oh Hanumanji! You are valiant and brave, with a body like lightening. You are the dispeller of darkness of evil thoughts and companion of good sense and wisdom.

Kanchan Baran Biraaj Subesaa, Kanan kundal kunchit kesa
Shri Hanumanji's physique is golden coloured. His dress is pretty, wearing 'Kundals' ear-rings and his hairs are long and curly.
Hath Bajra Aur Dhvaja Birjai, Kandhe Moonj Janeu saage.
Shri Hanumanji is holding in one hand a lighting bolt and in the other a banner with sacred threa d across his shoulder.
Shankar Suvna Kesari Nandan, Tej Pratap Maha Jag Vandan
Oh Hanumanji! You are the emanation of 'SHIVA' and you delight Shri Keshri. Being ever effulgent, you and hold vast sway over the universe. The entire world proptiates. You are adorable of all.
Vidyavaan Guni Ati Chatur, Ram Kaj Karibe Ko Atur
Oh! Shri Hanumanji! You are the repository learning, virtuous, very wise and highly keen to do the work of Shri Ram,
Prabhu Charittra Sun ibe Ko Rasiya, Ram Lakhan Sita man basyia.
You are intensely greedy for listening to the naration of Lord Ram's lifestory and revel on its enjoyment. You ever dwell in the hearts of Shri Ram-Sita and Shri Lakshman.
Sukshma roop Dhari Siyahi Dikhwana, Bikat roop Dhari Lank Jarawa
You appeared beofre Sita in a diminutive form and spoke to her, while you assumed an awesome form and struck terror by setting Lanka on fire.

Bhim roop Dhari Asur Sanhare, Ramchandra Ke kaaj Savare.
He, with his terrible form, killed demons in Lanka and performed all acts of Shri Ram.
Laye Sajivan Lakhan Jiyaye, Shri Raghubir harashi ur laye.
When Hanumanji made Lakshman alive after bringing 'Sanjivni herb' Shri Ram took him in his deep embrace, his heart full of joy.
Raghupati Kinhi Bahut Badaai, Tum Mama Priya Bharat Sam Bahi.
Shri Ram lustily extolled Hanumanji's excellence and remarked, "you are as dear to me as my own brother Bharat"
Sahastra Badan Tumharo Jas Gaave, Asa kahi Shripati Kanth Laagave.
Shri Ram embraced Hanumanji saying: "Let the thousand - tongued sheshnaag sing your glories"
Sankadik Brahmadi Muneesa, Narad Sarad Sahit Aheesa
Sanak and the sages, saints. Lord Brahma, the great hermits Narad and Goddess Saraswati along with Sheshnag the cosmic serpent, fail to sing the glories of Hanumanji exactly
Jam Kuber Digpal Jahan Te, Kabi Kabid Kahin Sake Kahan Te
What to talk of denizens of the earth like poets and scholars ones etc eve n Gods like Yamraj, Kuber, and Digpal fail to narrate Hanman's greatness in toto.
Tum Upkar Sugrivahi Keenha, Ram Miali Rajpad Deenha
Hanumanji! You rendered a great service for Sugriva, It were you who united him with SHRI RAM and installed him on the Royal Throne.

Tumharo Mantro Bibhishan Maana, Lankeshwar Bhaye Sab Jag Jaana.
By heeding your advice. Vibhushan became Lord of Lanka, which is known all over the universe.
Juug Sahastra Jojan Par Bhaanu, Leelyo Taahi Madhur Phal Jaanu
Hanumanji gulped, the SUN at distance of sixteen thousand miles considering it to be a sweet fruit.
Prabhu Mudrika Meli Mukha Maaheen, Jaladhi Langhi Gaye Acharaj Naheen.
Carrying the Lord's ring in his mouth, he went across the ocean. There is no wonder in that.
Durgam Kaaj Jagat Ke Jeete, Sugam Anugrah Tumhre Te Te.
Oh Hanumanji! all the difficult tasks in the world are rendered easiest by your grace.
Ram Duware Tum Rakhavare, Hot Na Aagya Bin Paisare.
Oh Hanumanji! You are the sentinel at the door of Ram's mercy mansion or His divine abode. No one may enter without your permission.
Sab Sukh Lahen Tumhari Sarna, Tum Rakshak Kaahu Ko Darnaa.
By your grace one can enjoy all happiness and one need not have any fear under your protection.
Aapan Tej Samharo Aapei, Tanau Lok Hank Te Kanpei
When you roar all the three worlds tremble and only you can control your might.

Bhoot Pisaach Nikat Nahi Avei, Mahabir Jab Naam Sunavei.
Great Brave on. Hanumanji's name keeps all the Ghosts, Demons & evils spirits away from his devotees.
Nasei Rog Hare Sab Peera, Japat Niranter Hanumant Beera
On reciting Hanumanji's holy name regularly all the maladies perish the entire pain disappears.
Sankat Te Hanuman Chhudavei, Man Kram Bachan Dhyan Jo Lavei.
Those who rembember Hanumanji in thought, word and deed are well guarded against their odds in life.
Sub Par Ram Tapasvee Raaja, Tinke Kaaj Sakal Tum Saaja
Oh Hanumanji! You are the caretaker of even Lord Rama, who has been hailed as the Supreme Lord and the Monarch of all those devoted in penances.
Aur Manorath Jo Koi Lave, Soi Amit Jivan Phal Pave.
Oh Hanumanji! You fulfill the desires of those who come to you and bestow the eternal nectar the highest fruit of life.
Charo Juung Partap Tumhara, Hai Parsiddha Jagat Ujiyara.
Oh Hanumanji! You magnificent glory is acclaimed far and wide all through the four ages and your fame is radianlty noted all over the cosmos.
Sadho Sant Ke Tum Rakhvare, Asur Nikandan Ram Dulare.
Oh Hanumanji! You are the saviour and the guardian angel of saints and sages and destroy all the Demons, you are the seraphic darling of Shri Ram.

Ashta Siddhi Nau Nidhi Ke Data, Asa Bar Din Janki Mata.
Hanumanji has been blessed with mother Janki to grant to any one any YOGIC power of eight Sidhis and Nava Nidhis as per choice.
Ram Rasayan Tumhare Pasa, Sadaa Raho Raghupati Ke Dasa.
Oh Hanumanji! You hold the essence of devotion to RAM, always rem aining His Servant.
Tumhare Bhajan Ramko Pavei. Janam Janam Ke Dukh Bisravei.
Oh Hanumanji! through devotion to you, one comes to RAM and becames free from suffering of several lives.
Anta Kaal Raghubar Pur Jai, Jahan Janma Hari Bhakta Kahai.
After death he enters the eternal abode of Sri Ram and remains a devotee of him, whenever, taking new birth on earth.
Aur Devata Chitt Na Dharai, Hanumant Sei Sarva Sukh Karai
You need not hold any other demigod in mind. Hanumanji alone will give all happiness.
Sankat Kate Mitey Sab Peera, Jo Sumirei Hanumant Balbeera
Oh Powerf ul Hanumanji! You end the sufferings and remove all the pain from those who remember you.
Jai Jai Jai Hanuman Gosai, Kripa Karahu Gurudev Ki Naiee
Hail-Hail-Hail-Lord Hanumanji! I beseech you Honour to bless me in the capacity of my supreme 'GURU' (teacher).

Jo Sat Baar Paath Kar Koi, Chhutahi Bandi Maha Sukh Hoi.
One who recites this Hanuman Chalisa one hundred times daily for one hundred days becames free from the bondage of life and death and ejoys the highest bliss at last.
Jo Yah Padhe Hanuman Chalisa, Hoy Siddhi Sakhi Gaurisa
As Lord Shankar witnesses, all those who recite Hanuman Chalisa regularly are sure to be benedicted
Tulsidas Sada Hari Chera, Keeje Nath Hriday Mah Dera.
Tulsidas always the servant of Lord prays. "Oh my Lord! You enshrine within my heart.!"
Chopai : Pavan Tanay Sankat Haran, Mangal Murti Roop, Ram Lakhan Sita Sahit, Hriday Basahu Sur Bhoop
O Shri Hanuman, The Son of Pavan, Saviour The Embodiment of blessings, reside in my heart together with Shri Ram, Laxman and Sita

History of Sunder Kand

The **Sunder Kand** is the fifth chapter of the Ramayana, authored by Maharishi Valmiki. It narrates the journey of Hanuman to Lanka in search of Sita. The word "Sunder" means beautiful, and this chapter is named so because it describes the virtues and divine actions of Hanuman, his unwavering devotion to Rama, and the triumph of good over evil.

Key events in Sunder Kand include:

1. **Hanuman's Leap Across the Ocean**: A demonstration of his unmatched strength, determination, and faith in Lord Rama.
2. **Meeting with Sita**: Hanuman consoles Sita, gives her Rama's message, and reinforces her hope.

3. **Burning of Lanka**: Hanuman, after being captured by Ravana, sets Lanka ablaze, signifying the ultimate destruction of arrogance and evil.
4. **Return to Rama**: Hanuman brings back the news of Sita, laying the foundation for the war between Rama and Ravana.

This chapter encapsulates the essence of faith, courage, and devotion, inspiring readers to overcome obstacles with resilience.

Why Sunder Kand is Recited During Emergencies

Sunder Kand is believed to hold immense spiritual power. Its recitation:

1. **Removes Obstacles**: It helps devotees navigate through challenges and distress.
2. **Strengthens Faith**: Reading the Sunder Kand instills a sense of courage and trust in divine intervention.
3. **Destroys Negative Energies**: The narrative of Hanuman's valor and devotion is said to dispel darkness and negativity.

Because of its potency, the Sunder Kand is often recited during times of great personal or familial crises, such as severe illness, financial difficulties, or spiritual despair. It is a call for divine aid, seeking the blessings of Hanuman and Rama to resolve dire situations.

Rules for Recitation

To ensure the sanctity and effectiveness of the Sunder Kand, devotees follow specific guidelines:

1. **Purity of Mind and Body**: Bathe and wear clean clothes before starting the recitation.
2. **Clean and Sacred Space**: Perform the reading in a quiet and pure environment, preferably near an altar or a designated place for worship.

3. **Devotional Attitude**: Approach the recitation with a calm mind and a heart filled with devotion.
4. **Fixed Time**: Recite it at the same time daily, preferably in the morning or evening.
5. **Avoid Interruption**: Once started, the recitation should not be interrupted or left incomplete.
6. **Observe Fasting or Restraints**: Some devotees fast or observe dietary restraints as an act of devotion.
7. **Use of Tulsi Mala**: A rosary made of Tulsi beads can be used to keep track of the verses or prayers.
8. **Chant Hanuman Chalisa Before and After**: Begin and conclude the session with the chanting of the Hanuman Chalisa for added devotion and blessings.

Reciting the Sunder Kand with faith and sincerity is believed to bring peace, resolve difficulties, and invoke divine protection and guidance.

Evidence and references about the existence of Hanuman stem from a mix of scriptural, historical, and cultural sources. Here's a summary of notable sources:

1. Scriptural References

- **Ramayana (Valmiki and other versions)**: Hanuman is a pivotal character, particularly in the Sundar Kand, which details his journey to Lanka, showcasing his strength, wisdom, and devotion.
- **Mahabharata**: Hanuman appears as Bhima's brother and blesses Arjuna's chariot during the Kurukshetra war.
- **Puranas**: Texts like the Vishnu Purana, Shiva Purana, and Skanda Purana reference Hanuman, affirming his divine nature and role in cosmic events.

2. Historical and Archaeological References

- **Anjanadri Hill (Kishkindha):** Believed to be Hanuman's birthplace, located near Hampi in Karnataka.
- **Hanuman Garhi, Ayodhya:** An ancient temple that links Ayodhya, Rama's birthplace, with Hanuman.
- **Sita Eliya, Sri Lanka:** Sites like Ashok Vatika and places in Sri Lanka claim connections to Hanuman's search for Sita.

3. Cultural and Regional Evidence

- **Hanuman Temples Worldwide:** Temples in India, Southeast Asia (e.g., Bali, Cambodia, Thailand), and even modern adaptations in the Caribbean and America show his enduring influence.
- **Folklore and Traditions:** Hanuman's stories are deeply ingrained in the oral traditions of various cultures, often aligned with local geographical markers.
- **Indonesian Ramayana:** Reliefs and sculptures of Hanuman in temples like Prambanan attest to his revered status beyond India.

4. Scientific and Rational Inquiries

- **Floating Rocks in Rameswaram:** Some associate these with Hanuman's monkey army building the Ram Setu. Modern science has studied their unique density and floating characteristics.
- **Ram Setu (Adam's Bridge):** Satellite imagery showing a submerged bridge connecting India and Sri Lanka aligns with descriptions in the Ramayana.

5. Philosophical and Devotional Impact

- **Hanuman Chalisa:** Written by Tulsidas, this 40-verse hymn reflects Hanuman's qualities and is widely revered.

- **Astrological and Yogic Traditions**: Hanuman is seen as a patron of strength, intellect, and devotion, influencing spiritual practices.

While definitive archaeological evidence of Hanuman's existence as a historical figure remains elusive, the extensive scriptural, cultural, and geographical references continue to inspire faith and devotion.

Chapter 3:
The Story Behind Jyotirlingas and their Importance

Jyotirlingas hold a special place in Hindu mythology and spirituality. These twelve sacred shrines of Lord Shiva are believed to be manifestations of his infinite light and cosmic energy. The word "Jyotirlinga" comes from two Sanskrit words: "Jyoti" (light) and "Linga" (symbol of Shiva). Together, it signifies the radiance of the divine form of Shiva.

The Origin of Jyotirlingas

The story of the Jyotirlingas is rooted in an ancient episode from the Shiva Purana. Once, there was a debate between Lord Brahma and Lord Vishnu over who was superior. As the argument escalated, a massive pillar of light appeared before them, stretching infinitely into the heavens and the depths of the earth. Both deities decided to determine its origin and end.

- **Brahma** took the form of a swan and flew upwards, seeking the pinnacle of the light.
- **Vishnu** transformed into a boar and dug deep into the earth, trying to find its base.

After a futile search, they returned, unable to find the beginning or end of the light. At that moment, Lord Shiva emerged from the pillar, revealing that it symbolized his infinite and omnipresent nature. This divine pillar of light is considered the first Jyotirlinga, representing Shiva's transcendental presence.

The Twelve Jyotirlingas

Each of the twelve Jyotirlingas has its own unique story and significance, symbolizing different aspects of Lord Shiva's power and compassion. The twelve are:

1. **Somnath (Gujarat):** Known as the "Protector of the Moon God," this shrine commemorates Shiva's role in restoring the waning moon.

2. **Mallikarjuna (Andhra Pradesh):** Located on Shri Shaila Mountain, this Jyotirlinga represents Shiva and Parvati's eternal union.

3. **Mahakaleshwar (Madhya Pradesh):** Revered as the Lord of Time, it is believed to provide liberation from the cycle of life and death.

4. **Omkareshwar (Madhya Pradesh):** Situated on an island shaped like the sacred "Om" symbol, this Jyotirlinga signifies Shiva's cosmic energy.

5. **Kedarnath (Uttarakhand):** Nestled in the Himalayas, this shrine represents Shiva as the protector of the universe.

6. **Bhimashankar (Maharashtra):** Known for destroying the demon Tripurasura, this Jyotirlinga symbolizes Shiva's victory over evil.

7. **Kashi Vishwanath (Uttar Pradesh):** Located in Varanasi, this Jyotirlinga represents liberation and spiritual enlightenment.

8. **Trimbakeshwar (Maharashtra):** Associated with the origin of the sacred Godavari River, it signifies the cleansing of sins.

9. **Vaidyanath (Jharkhand):** Known as the "Doctor of the Gods," this Jyotirlinga is associated with healing and well-being.

10. **Nageshwar (Gujarat):** Representing protection from poison, this Jyotirlinga reminds devotees of Shiva's protective nature.

11. **Rameshwaram (Tamil Nadu):** Associated with Lord Rama's devotion to Shiva, this Jyotirlinga highlights the importance of faith and penance.

12. **Grishneshwar (Maharashtra):** Known as the "Lord of Compassion," it symbolizes Shiva's benevolence and forgiveness.

Importance of Jyotirlinga Worship

1. **Spiritual Awakening:** Worshiping at Jyotirlingas is believed to help devotees attain self-realization and liberation (moksha).
2. **Purification of Karma:** Each Jyotirlinga is considered a center of energy that purifies past deeds and aligns devotees with divine grace.
3. **Cosmic Connection:** The Jyotirlingas serve as a bridge between the physical and spiritual realms, offering a sense of unity with the cosmos.
4. **Cultural Significance:** Each shrine reflects regional traditions and architectural marvels, showcasing the diversity of India's spiritual heritage.

Rules and Rituals for Worship

To fully benefit from the divine vibrations of the Jyotirlingas, devotees follow specific rituals:

- **Purity of Body and Mind:** Devotees cleanse themselves physically and mentally before entering the temple.
- **Offerings:** Traditional offerings include Bilva leaves, water, milk, and flowers, which hold symbolic significance.
- **Chanting of Mantras:** Reciting the "Om Namah Shivaya" mantra enhances the spiritual experience.
- **Circumambulation:** Devotees perform "parikrama" around the sanctum sanctorum, moving in a clockwise direction.

Eternal Light of Devotion

The Jyotirlingas are not just physical shrines but profound symbols of eternal light and spiritual energy. They remind devotees of Lord Shiva's boundless compassion, infinite power, and all-pervading presence. By understanding their significance, we deepen our connection to the divine and reaffirm our faith in the ultimate truth.

MY PERSONAL EXPERIENCE IN MAHAKALESHWAR TEMPLE

It was during a particularly challenging time in my life that I found myself drawn to Mahakaleshwar, the sacred temple dedicated to Lord Shiva. The weight of the world seemed to rest on my shoulders, and everything felt overwhelming. I was searching for peace, for a sign that everything would eventually be okay. The journey to Mahakaleshwar felt like a desperate plea for guidance.

I arrived at the temple in Ujjain, where the air was thick with spirituality. The sound of bells ringing in the distance and the chants of devotees filled the atmosphere. I entered the temple with a sense of reverence, feeling a strange mix of anxiety and hope.

As I walked through the temple, I noticed the offerings—flowers, incense, and bhang—an intoxicating herbal drink associated with Lord Shiva. In a moment of surrender, I decided to partake in the bhang, hoping it would bring clarity to my troubled mind.

After consuming it, the world around me began to fade. The noise of the crowd seemed to melt away, and I found myself in a state of trance. I could feel the presence of something beyond the physical, something divine, as if I was in direct communion with Lord Shiva himself.

It wasn't just a hallucination; it felt real—tangible. In that state, I felt the weight of all my struggles lift. It was as if Shiva was speaking to me, telling me that life's trials were just passing phases, meant to teach me lessons of strength, patience, and wisdom. I could sense the eternal truth that everything, no matter how dark, eventually leads to light. There was a sense of deep connection, of understanding, that I had never experienced before.

Lord Shiva, in that moment, became my anchor. He reassured me that my pain was not forever. He reminded me of the power of self-determination, of how to stay grounded in faith and perseverance. I felt a profound sense of peace, as though I had been seen, heard, and understood by the very force that governs the universe.

When I woke from the trance-like state, I felt a wave of calm wash over me. The chaos in my mind had settled. As I left the temple, the world seemed different. I carried a renewed sense of purpose, a quiet confidence that my struggles would soon pass and that I was never truly alone.

In the days that followed, things began to change. My relationships improved, my mindset shifted from one of despair to hope, and opportunities began to unfold. The challenges I faced no longer felt like insurmountable obstacles, but rather lessons that I was ready to face with resilience and strength. I could feel the blessings of Lord Shiva guiding me through.

It was as if, through that experience at Mahakaleshwar, I had not just visited a temple, but had also connected with the eternal divine, transforming my life in ways I could never have imagined. My journey became a testament to the fact that, sometimes, when you surrender to the divine, life has a way of unfolding in the most unexpected and beautiful ways.

After my transformative experience at Mahakaleshwar, I found myself captivated by the temple's sacred energy. Mahakaleshwar is not just a place of worship; it is one of the most powerful Jyotirlingas, where Lord Shiva's divine presence is believed to be eternal and unshakable. Situated in Ujjain, this ancient temple holds a unique significance in Hindu spirituality, and I began to understand why it was revered by millions.

Mahakaleshwar is said to be the abode of the "Mahakal," or the Great Lord of Time, who controls the cycles of creation, preservation, and destruction in the universe. It is believed that Lord Shiva in this form governs both life and death, offering his protection from the destructive forces of time. This made me realize that my own struggles, though overwhelming at the time, were part of the grand cosmic plan, and in the presence of Mahakaleshwar, I felt connected to a power much larger than myself—something eternal, that existed beyond the human experience.

It was during my stay at the temple that I was fortunate enough to witness the *Bhasma Aarti*, a ritual that is an absolute must-see for any devotee. The Bhasma Aarti is performed early in the morning, before sunrise, and is one of the most unique and sacred rituals associated with Mahakaleshwar. The temple priests use sacred ash (*bhasma*) to perform the aarti, symbolizing the cycle of life, death, and rebirth. The ash signifies the impermanence of life, reminding us that everything material is transient.

As I stood there watching the ceremony unfold, I felt as though I was standing in the presence of Lord Shiva himself. The devotion in the air was palpable; the chanting of Vedic hymns, the ringing of bells, and the sight of the priest waving the sacred flame made it clear that this was not just an ordinary ritual—it was a divine connection, a direct channel to the almighty. The sight of the sacred ash being offered to the deity felt like a profound reminder that life, with all its challenges and hardships, is but a part of the eternal cycle. Everything, even death, is a part of Lord Shiva's creation, and it all leads to transformation and liberation.

I closed my eyes for a moment during the Bhasma Aarti, and in that brief pause, I felt an immense spiritual awakening. The rituals, the prayers, and the devotion all came together, filling me with a sense of divine presence. It was as if Lord Shiva himself was embracing me, guiding me through my troubles and offering me his strength and wisdom.

The sound of the bells and the rhythmic chants seemed to penetrate deep within me, allowing me to let go of the weight I had been carrying. I could feel Shiva's essence all around me, within me, guiding my every step. It was in that moment that I truly understood that Lord Shiva, with his infinite grace, is not just a distant god; he is ever-present, accessible to those who seek him with an open heart.

The experience left me feeling renewed. I had been connected not just to a place or a ritual, but to the very spirit of Lord Shiva. I could feel his eternal power, his understanding of time, and his ability to heal. The Bhasma Aarti, with its deep symbolism and reverence, became a bridge for me to connect directly with the divine.

From that day onwards, my life took on a different rhythm. The worries that once seemed insurmountable now felt like challenges I could face with Shiva's blessings. I found myself carrying the peace I had gained at Mahakaleshwar into my everyday life. I knew that I was not alone, that Shiva's eternal presence was with me, guiding me through the highs and lows, offering me the strength to endure, and the wisdom to transcend. The *Bhasma Aarti* had not only deepened my connection to Lord Shiva but also transformed the way I saw my life and my place in the universe.

Chapter 4 :
The Sacred Shakti Peeths and the Divine Feminine Power

In the sacred lore of Hinduism, the concept of Shakti, the divine feminine energy, holds a revered place. It is said that the universe itself is driven by Shakti, the source of all power and creation. The story behind the formation of Shakti Peeths, the sacred shrines dedicated to the Goddess, is one of love, loss, and the eternal connection between the divine feminine and masculine forces.

The origin of the Shakti Peeths is intricately linked to the myth of the goddess Sati, the first wife of Lord Shiva. According to ancient texts, Sati, the daughter of the great king Daksha, fell in love with Lord Shiva, a simple ascetic who resided in the mountains, meditating in deep solitude. Despite her father's disapproval of Shiva, Sati married him, driven by her deep devotion and love.

However, Daksha, in his arrogance and pride, organized a grand yajna (sacrifice) but intentionally did not invite his daughter and son-in-law. Feeling insulted and hurt by this omission, Sati decided to attend the yajna alone to confront her father. She hoped that the power of her presence would compel Daksha to recognize her as his daughter, but when she arrived, Daksha's disregard for her husband, Lord Shiva, was more evident than ever. In his mockery and disrespect towards Shiva, Daksha's actions triggered deep sorrow within Sati.

Unable to bear the humiliation, Sati, in her grief and anger, decided to end her life by self-immolation. Her body was consumed by the flames of her own sacrifice, and her soul left the mortal world. Upon hearing the news of her demise, Lord Shiva was overcome with grief and rage. In his anguish, he performed the *Tandav*, a furious dance of destruction. Shiva's sorrow was so immense that the very balance of the universe seemed to tremble.

To bring an end to the destruction, Lord Vishnu intervened. He used his Sudarshan Chakra to cut Sati's body into pieces. As the body was dismembered, the pieces of Sati's body fell to various places on Earth, and each of these spots became a sacred Shakti Peeth. These places are where the divine presence of the Goddess is believed to manifest, signifying the undying love and devotion between Sati and Shiva.

Each of these 51 Shakti Peeths is associated with one of the body parts or ornaments of Sati. They are spread across India and beyond, and each one holds immense significance, both spiritually and historically. The sacredness of these shrines makes them places of deep devotion and reverence for millions of followers of the Goddess in her various forms.

The Importance of Shakti Peeths

Shakti Peeths are not just physical locations but are considered gateways to the divine feminine energy. They represent the power of the Goddess in her many forms, from Durga, the warrior goddess, to Kali, the destroyer, to Lakshmi, the goddess of wealth, and Saraswati, the goddess of knowledge. These peeths symbolize the belief that the universe is governed not just by the masculine principle of creation and destruction, but also by the nurturing, creative, and transformative power of the feminine.

The importance of the Shakti Peeths lies in their ability to connect the devotee to the cosmic energy of Shakti. It is said that by visiting these sacred shrines, one can invoke the goddess's blessings, which provide strength, protection, wisdom, and prosperity. These temples serve as reminders of the delicate balance between the masculine and feminine energies, both within the universe and within oneself.

At these holy sites, it is believed that the goddess is present in her full divine form, and devotees who offer sincere prayers are granted her divine grace. Pilgrims travel from all corners of the world to visit the Shakti Peeths, hoping to experience the transformative power of the Goddess and to seek her guidance in times of need.

Key Shakti Peeths

1. **Kamakhya Temple (Assam)**: Located in the hills of Assam, Kamakhya is one of the most famous Shakti Peeths. It is dedicated to the goddess Kamakhya, an aspect of Sati, and is renowned for its association with fertility and tantric worship.

2. **Vaishno Devi Temple (Jammu & Kashmir)**: Situated in the Trikuta Mountains, this temple is dedicated to Goddess Vaishno, another form of the Goddess Durga. The temple attracts millions of pilgrims each year who come to seek blessings for strength and protection.

3. **Kalighat Temple (Kolkata)**: This temple is dedicated to Goddess Kali, the fierce and powerful form of Shakti. The temple's significance is rooted in Kali's power to destroy evil and create transformation.

4. **Jwalamukhi Temple (Himachal Pradesh)**: Dedicated to Goddess Jwala, this temple is known for its natural gas flames that burn perpetually, symbolizing the goddess's fire and energy.

5. **Shakti Peeth in Puri (Odisha)**: Known for its connection to Goddess Sati's body parts, this peeth is an important place of pilgrimage for followers of the Shakta tradition.

6. **Saptashrungi Temple (Maharashtra)**: Nestled in the mountains, this temple is dedicated to Goddess Saptashrungi, another revered form of the divine feminine, and is an important site for spiritual seekers.

Connection to the Divine Feminine

The Shakti Peeths are more than just sacred destinations; they represent a journey into the heart of the divine feminine. The destruction of Sati's body and the dispersal of her sacred parts across the earth symbolize the fact that the goddess, like energy itself, is ever-present. The pieces of her body, scattered across the land, are reminders of the goddess's eternal essence and her ability to sustain the universe through her diverse forms.

Visiting a Shakti Peeth is not merely a ritual; it is a way to connect to the cosmic energy of the Goddess, to understand the divine forces that govern creation, and to honor the eternal dance of life and death, creation and destruction. The Shakti Peeths remind us that the power of the universe is not only masculine but also deeply feminine, nurtured and sustained by the Goddess.

In my own life, understanding the significance of these Shakti Peeths has brought a sense of balance and empowerment. It has shown me that both masculine and feminine energies coexist within all beings, and it is through embracing this balance that we find true strength, transformation, and spiritual connection.

Chapter 5:
The Toe Ring—A Symbol of Tradition and its Hidden Power

When I first got married, there were many customs and rituals that I was expected to embrace. Some I welcomed with open arms, while others felt unfamiliar and, to be honest, somewhat uncomfortable. One such custom that I found difficult to accept was wearing the *toe ring*.

At the time of my wedding, my mother-in-law, like many others, handed me a small silver ring, meant to be worn on the second toe of my left foot. She explained that it was a customary piece of jewelry for married women, much like the mangalsutra or the sindoor. But I remember feeling quite uneasy about it. I had always associated toe rings with a specific image of tradition that seemed outdated and restrictive, and I didn't see any reason to wear something that felt uncomfortable.

Despite my reluctance, I wore the toe ring out of respect for the tradition and the people who cared about me. However, I couldn't help but feel that it was just another piece of jewelry, a mere ornament that didn't serve much purpose other than adhering to the ritualistic aspects of marriage. I wondered why something as simple as a toe ring had to hold so much significance, especially in today's world, where I was striving for independence and modernity.

But life has a way of surprising us, and soon after I began wearing the toe ring, I started to notice subtle changes in my body. At first, I dismissed them as coincidences, but gradually, I began to realize that there might be something more to this tradition than I had initially thought.

The Revelation: Discovering the Science Behind the Toe Ring

One day, while browsing through an old book on Ayurvedic traditions, I stumbled upon a section about the health benefits of wearing a toe ring. The information piqued my curiosity. According to ancient wisdom, the second toe on the left foot is connected to the *Uterus* and *Reproductive System,* specifically the *ovaries* through the nervous system. The toe ring, which was typically made of silver, was said to have a special role in balancing and regulating energy in the body, especially for women.

It turns out that wearing a toe ring, traditionally, wasn't just a cultural practice—it was rooted in the science of acupressure and energy channels. The toe ring, when worn on the second toe of the left foot, was believed to help in maintaining hormonal balance. The gentle pressure exerted by the ring on the toe was thought to activate specific acupressure points that influence the reproductive system. The result, according to the teachings, was a positive effect on menstrual cycles, fertility, and even overall well-being.

I also read that silver, being a highly conductive metal, has properties that help regulate body temperature and maintain balance in the body. Silver was believed to absorb negative energy, which could otherwise cause imbalance. The toe ring, in this context, wasn't just a symbol of marriage but also a tool for health and spiritual harmony.

The more I learned, the more I realized that the toe ring was not just a simple piece of jewelry; it was an ancient tool designed to promote balance in a woman's life—physically, emotionally, and spiritually. This ancient practice was not based on superstition, but rather on a deep understanding of the human body and its connection to the universe.

Embracing the Tradition: Finding Harmony

As I delved deeper into the understanding of this tradition, I began to wear my toe ring with a newfound sense of respect. It became more than just an ornament; it became a daily reminder of the sacred connection between my body and mind. I started to appreciate the wisdom embedded in this custom—how it wasn't just about maintaining the outward appearance of marriage, but about nurturing my health and well-being in ways I hadn't fully understood before.

Over time, I began to notice subtle improvements in my health. I felt more grounded and balanced, and my menstrual cycle, which had been irregular in the past, started to stabilize. It wasn't an instant miracle, but I could sense a gradual change in my physical and emotional state. I felt more connected to my body, more in tune with the natural rhythms of life.

As I continued wearing the toe ring, I realized that it was a simple yet profound way of embracing my feminine energy and honoring the connection between body, mind, and spirit. I felt empowered by the knowledge that this tradition, passed down through generations, was not just about adhering to customs, but about aligning with the deeper forces of nature.

The Larger Perspective: Traditions and Their Hidden Wisdom

Looking back, I now understand that many of the traditions I once questioned were rooted in ancient wisdom—wisdom that was not always immediately clear but had been preserved through generations. These practices, whether it's the toe ring, the mangalsutra, or other rituals, are not just symbolic but often carry hidden wisdom that connects us to the natural world and its energies.

The toe ring, in particular, taught me that traditions should not be blindly followed or dismissed. They deserve to be understood and respected for the knowledge they carry. In today's fast-paced world, we often overlook these subtle, yet powerful, practices. But when we take the time to learn about them, we find that they can enrich our lives in ways we never imagined.

For me, the toe ring became a symbol of balance, a tangible connection to the ancient wisdom of Ayurveda, and a reminder of my own journey of self-discovery. Through it, I learned to honor not just the customs of marriage, but the deeper energies that shape our lives, empowering me to lead a more harmonious and fulfilled life.

And so, I wear my toe ring not out of obligation, but with gratitude—grateful for the knowledge it brought into my life and the new understanding it gave me about the interconnectedness of body, mind, and spirit.

Chapter 6:
Piercings – The Painful Yet Meaningful Journey

As a child, I always dreaded the thought of getting my nose and ears pierced. It was a rite of passage in my family, a tradition passed down through generations. Every girl in our family had their ears and nose pierced early on, and it was expected of me to follow suit. However, to me, the thought of needles and the sharp pain that would follow was terrifying. The mere idea of someone piercing my skin seemed unbearable, and I dreaded the moment it would inevitably arrive.

I vividly remember the day when my mother took me to the local jeweler, who also doubled as a piercer. I was probably around eight or nine years old, and the thought of getting my ears pierced already filled me with dread. My heart raced with each step we took toward the shop. My mother, smiling as though she had experienced this numerous times, tried to calm me down, but nothing could ease my anxiety. She reassured me that it was a common practice and that I would feel better once it was done.

As I sat on the small wooden chair, the piercing specialist brought out a small needle and a shiny piece of gold jewelry for my ears. I closed my eyes tightly, unable to look at the process. The first sharp sting made me wince and cry out in pain. It felt like a burning sensation, and I was sure it would last forever. But it was over in a flash, and before I could even fully process the pain, the second piercing was done.

The discomfort didn't stop there. Soon after, the wounds started to throb, and I had to deal with the aftercare. Cleaning the piercings with antiseptic solution and ensuring they didn't get infected made the process feel like a never-ending cycle of irritation. Despite the pain, my family reassured me that it was for a greater purpose. They explained that ear piercings were considered an important ritual for young girls, marking their entry into womanhood, and that they would bring good health, strength, and beauty.

But what I hadn't anticipated was the experience of getting my nose pierced. I remember resisting it fiercely, even crying at the thought of it. My mother, though understanding of my fear, was insistent, explaining that the nose piercing was a traditional practice in our family and held significant cultural value. In many cultures, it is believed that nose piercings not only enhance beauty but also have medicinal benefits. They are believed to balance a woman's physical and mental well-being, aligning with the ancient practice of acupuncture, where specific pressure points on the body are stimulated to promote health.

When the piercing needle went through my nose, the pain felt even more intense than the ear piercings. It was sharp and stinging, making my eyes tear up instantly. But just as with the ears, it didn't last long, and soon I was left with the small silver ring in my nose. The pain gradually subsided, but the discomfort of cleaning the new piercing remained, and I often found myself worrying about whether it would get infected or cause any problems.

As I grew older, the significance of these piercings began to unfold before me. I learned that the nose piercing, particularly on the left nostril, is believed to have health benefits. In Ayurvedic traditions, it is said that the left side of the nose is connected to the reproductive organs, and piercing it can help alleviate menstrual pain, regulate the menstrual cycle, and enhance fertility. This ancient belief made me realize that my nose piercing wasn't just a symbol of tradition, but a part of a holistic practice intended to help maintain my physical and emotional well-being.

As for the ear piercings, I came to understand their cultural importance as well. They are not just a sign of femininity and beauty but also hold spiritual significance. In many cultures, it is believed that the act of piercing the ears opens up the energy channels, allowing for the free flow of life energy (prana). This was reinforced by the fact that ear piercings are also believed to improve hearing and enhance mental clarity, helping to strengthen the mind and senses. Over time, I began to see these piercings as more than mere ornaments; they were a form of self-care, a ritual designed to help me stay connected to my body and mind.

As I embraced the significance of these piercings, I found myself feeling more empowered. The pain and discomfort I had once dreaded had transformed into a reminder of strength and resilience. These piercings, which had once felt like an imposition, became a symbol of my growth and understanding. They were no longer just physical marks; they were part of a deeper spiritual and cultural practice that had been passed down to me.

Through the years, as I learned more about the science and the symbolism behind the piercings, I realized that they weren't just a ritual that was imposed on me—they were gifts that connected me to generations of women who had walked this path before me. The pain of the needle, the discomfort of healing, and the occasional annoyance of aftercare were all small prices to pay for the profound sense of connection I now felt to my culture, my body, and my feminine energy.

Looking back, I no longer view those piercings as a painful initiation into womanhood. Instead, I see them as an important part of my journey—a journey that has taught me to embrace not only the traditions of my ancestors but also the deeper wisdom that lies beneath the surface. The discomfort that once seemed unbearable has given way to understanding, and in that understanding, I have found peace and strength.

Chapter 7:
The Unseen Power of Tradition – Understanding the Restrictions During My Periods

As a young girl, I found it difficult to understand the practice of not being allowed to participate in religious rituals or worship during my periods. It was something I had grown up with—my mother would gently but firmly tell me that during those days, I was not allowed to enter the temple or even engage in certain pujas and prayers at home. At first, I accepted it as just another one of those family traditions that I had to follow without question, but as I grew older, I started to feel a sense of injustice and frustration.

Why was it that, during a time when I needed emotional comfort and spiritual connection the most, I was told to refrain from worshiping? It seemed paradoxical to me that a time of intense physical and emotional change, where I felt disconnected from my body and often overwhelmed by my emotions, was precisely when I was restricted from seeking solace in spirituality. I couldn't understand why a natural biological process, something that every woman goes through, should have any bearing on her ability to pray or worship.

I vividly remember the many times I would watch my family perform poojas or go to the temple while I sat on the sidelines, feeling isolated. As a teenager, it felt like a punishment. The other women in the house would explain that it was because women were considered "impure" during their periods, and there were certain customs that dictated how one should conduct oneself during this time. I would hear my elders talk about how a woman in this state was not supposed to enter sacred spaces or engage in rituals, and I would feel a deep sense of alienation.

It wasn't just about the physical act of worship; it was the emotional and spiritual connection I had with it. Being told that I couldn't offer prayers during my periods left me feeling excluded and unworthy of participating in something so integral to my sense of identity and faith. I used to question the fairness of it, wondering why something so natural and biological should have such a strong hold over my ability to express my devotion to God.

As time passed, I became increasingly disillusioned with the idea that my body's natural cycles could somehow disqualify me from worship. But little did I know that this frustration would soon lead me on a journey of self-discovery—one that would open my eyes to the deeper significance of the tradition and the wisdom hidden behind it.

During one of my visits to a spiritual retreat, I happened to meet a wise woman, an experienced spiritual practitioner, who spoke to me about the science behind the restrictions that had always baffled me. She began by explaining that many traditions and customs, although they may appear as societal rules or prohibitions, often have deep-rooted scientific and psychological bases.

She explained that during menstruation, a woman's body undergoes a series of physical, hormonal, and emotional changes that can make her more sensitive and susceptible to energy fluctuations. This period of hormonal imbalance, she told me, affects not only the body but also the mind and spirit. According to ancient wisdom, the menstrual cycle is viewed as a time when a woman's energy is redirected inward, towards self-healing and introspection. During this time, it is believed that women are more spiritually attuned to their inner selves but also more vulnerable to external energies.

In the past, when medical science had not yet advanced, there was a belief that a woman's immune system was weaker during menstruation. Thus, to prevent her from becoming exposed to harmful energies or pathogens in sacred spaces, rituals were designed to protect her well-being. In this context, refraining from entering the temple or participating in communal worship was seen as a way to shield her from external influences that could disrupt her natural balance.

Moreover, the spiritual side of this restriction is rooted in the idea of sanctity. Temples and holy spaces are believed to be charged with powerful energy, and it was thought that during menstruation, a woman's aura might be fluctuating due to hormonal and emotional changes. It was believed that this could disturb the energy of the space, and so it was best to allow her the time to heal and restore her own energy before re-entering the sacred space.

Another aspect of this tradition is the practice of allowing a woman to rest during her periods. While menstruation is not an illness, it is a time of physical exertion, with blood loss and hormonal changes that can lead to fatigue and discomfort. The restriction on worship was, in part, a way of allowing women to focus on their physical needs—rest, nourishment, and self-care—without the added pressure of religious duties.

The more I learned, the more I realized that these practices were not about discrimination or punishment but about honoring a woman's body and her energy. They were rooted in ancient wisdom that sought to protect her well-being, both physically and spiritually, during a time when her body needed rest and recuperation.

Over time, I began to see the sense in these traditions. The concept of spiritual and physical energy being interconnected made much more sense to me. I understood that the practice of not worshiping during menstruation was not about exclusion, but about allowing women the space to conserve their energy and find balance within themselves before reconnecting with the divine. It was a time for inner reflection and self-care—an opportunity to focus on healing, both physically and emotionally.

What once seemed like an outdated and oppressive rule now felt like a protective practice designed with wisdom. The restrictions weren't about holding women back from their faith, but rather about guiding them to understand their own natural rhythms and the importance of taking care of themselves during vulnerable times. The wisdom embedded in this tradition reminded me that spirituality is not just about performing rituals but also about nurturing the body and the mind.

From that point forward, I no longer felt offended or isolated by the tradition. Instead, I embraced it as a time for self-reflection and inner peace. I began to see menstruation not as a burden or a restriction but as an opportunity to focus inward, to connect with myself, and to restore my energy before engaging with the world around me. The sense of exclusion I had once felt was replaced by a deep sense of respect for the natural processes of my body and the ancient traditions that guided me to honour them.

In the end, what had once been a source of frustration became a profound lesson in self-care, spirituality, and the wisdom of tradition. It taught me that sometimes, what seems like a restriction is actually a means of protection—a way to preserve our energy, our health, and our connection to the divine.

Chapter 8:
The Dilemma of Sindoor – Unraveling the Mystery Behind Tradition

Growing up in a traditional family, there were certain practices that I accepted without question, simply because they had always been a part of my life. One such practice that always intrigued me, yet left me in a constant state of confusion, was the application of sindoor, the red powder worn by married women along the parting of their hair. As a young girl, I never quite understood why it was a symbol reserved exclusively for married women. Why was sindoor, with its bright red hue, applied only by women, and not by men or unmarried women? Was it merely a tradition, a cultural norm, or was there something deeper, something more significant behind it?

The first time I asked my mother why sindoor was applied only by married women, her answer was simple: "It is a sign of a woman's marital status. It signifies that she is married and symbolizes the sacred bond between her and her husband." While I understood the social aspect of it—how it marked the woman as married—I couldn't help but feel that there must be more to it than just a social marker. Why was this practice so deeply ingrained in our culture? And why, out of all the symbols, was sindoor chosen to represent marriage? These were the questions that kept swirling in my mind, leaving me in a dilemma.

I had grown up with the belief that sindoor was primarily an outward expression of a woman's devotion to her husband, a visible sign that her marital bond was sacred and unbreakable. But this explanation never fully satisfied me. Why should a woman's status be tied to a powder applied to her forehead? And more importantly, what about the significance of the color red, and why was it so specific to women?

The dilemma continued to haunt me, especially when I saw women from different backgrounds applying sindoor in varying ways, each with their own set of customs and beliefs. Some women applied it just at the hairline, while others would apply it to the forehead as well. The variations seemed endless, but one thing was constant: it was always the women who wore sindoor. As a young, curious girl, I began to question if this practice was rooted in something more profound, something beyond the realms of tradition and cultural norms.

It wasn't until later in my life, when I started to explore the deeper meanings behind traditional practices, that I uncovered the scientific reasons behind the use of sindoor. It was during a discussion with a spiritual guide and some knowledgeable elders that I began to connect the dots. What I discovered was that the practice of applying sindoor was not just a superficial act, but had a deeply scientific and spiritual significance.

Sindoor, as it turns out, is made from a combination of natural ingredients, including vermilion (a red powder), which contains a mineral called mercury (also known as "sindoor" in its natural form). For centuries, this red powder has been used as a part of spiritual rituals, and it was found that the chemical properties of mercury had certain benefits, especially when applied to the skin in small, controlled amounts.

The first explanation that resonated with me was related to the concept of *bindi* or *third eye*. Applying sindoor to the forehead, specifically to the area just above the eyebrows, corresponds to the spot that is believed to be the location of the third eye in spiritual traditions. The third eye, or *ajna chakra*, is associated with intuition, perception, and higher consciousness. It is said that when the sindoor is applied to this spot, it helps stimulate the third eye, enhancing clarity and spiritual insight. The act of applying sindoor, in this sense, becomes an offering to one's inner wisdom and a way of aligning oneself with higher consciousness.

But the scientific aspect of sindoor goes beyond just spiritual symbolism. Mercury, when applied in small quantities, is believed to have a therapeutic effect on the body. In Ayurveda, it is considered that applying sindoor on the forehead helps regulate body temperature, balances hormones, and promotes mental clarity. The practice of applying sindoor was also linked to the regulation of blood circulation in the body. This was something I had never considered before. What was once simply a cultural symbol was now revealed to have roots in science and wellness.

The practice of applying sindoor to the parting of the hair, traditionally a woman's domain, also has its significance. The hair, according to Ayurveda and other spiritual traditions, is believed to hold energy channels that connect us to our inner self and the universe. The application of sindoor on the parting of the hair is said to harmonize the body's energy and create balance within. It is believed to enhance a woman's vitality and protect her from negative energies. Furthermore, the practice of applying sindoor to this area is thought to connect the woman to her feminine energy, which has always been considered sacred and powerful.

Another scientific aspect I learned was how the practice of applying sindoor may have roots in the concept of acupuncture. The forehead, being an acupressure point, is an area rich in nerve endings and blood vessels. When sindoor is applied to this region, it is believed to stimulate the energy flow, bringing health benefits, both mental and physical. It's a way of channeling energy and activating important nerve centers in the body. The application of sindoor, therefore, not only serves a spiritual purpose but also has the potential to affect the body's physiology in a positive way.

As I delved deeper into the origins of sindoor and its cultural and scientific significance, my perspective began to shift. I realized that the tradition, though seemingly simple and ceremonial, was based on a deeper understanding of the body, the mind, and the spirit. It wasn't about marking a woman as "belonging" to someone else, as I had once thought, but rather about recognizing the woman's connection to herself, her partner, and the universe.

Sindoor, with its red color, symbolizes not just the sacred bond of marriage but also vitality, energy, and spiritual awakening. The practice had been designed to help women remain connected to their own energy and wisdom, while also promoting their health and well-being. What was once a mystery to me—a simple cultural ritual—had unfolded into a beautiful, multi-layered practice that intertwined science, spirituality, and tradition.

By the time I came to understand the scientific and spiritual significance behind sindoor, I no longer viewed it as a mere mark of marital status. It had transformed in my mind into a powerful symbol of womanhood, energy, and inner strength. I wore it with newfound respect, appreciating its deep connection to my own energy, and realizing that sometimes, traditions that seem superficial may carry profound wisdom behind them.

Chapter 9:
The Significance of Going Barefoot in a Temple

In every corner of the world, temples stand as sacred spaces of worship, where people come together to seek blessings, offer prayers, and connect with the divine. As a child, I always noticed that one common practice across all temples was the tradition of going barefoot. It seemed so natural to me that I never really questioned it. It was just something we did. However, as I grew older and began to think more critically about the rituals and practices surrounding religious spaces, I started wondering: why do we go barefoot in a temple?

At first, the answer seemed quite straightforward. It was simply part of the tradition. However, as I delved deeper into the significance of this practice, I began to understand that there is much more to it than a mere cultural custom. Going barefoot in a temple, it turns out, is a practice that carries spiritual, scientific, and even energetic significance.

The first aspect that caught my attention was the spiritual reasoning behind this tradition. In many cultures and religions, the act of going barefoot is considered an offering of humility and respect. It is a way of acknowledging the sacredness of the space we are entering. The idea is that by removing our footwear, we leave behind any dirt, dust, and ego that may have accumulated in the outside world. We step into the temple as humble beings, acknowledging that we are in the presence of the divine, and we are not superior to the sacred space we are entering.

In Hinduism, the earth is considered sacred, and every step taken on it is thought to carry spiritual significance. The ground beneath our feet is seen as a conduit for energy, and by going barefoot, we are thought to be connecting more deeply with the earth's energies. This practice helps us attune ourselves to the spiritual vibrations that reside in the temple and the earth itself. The physical act of touching the ground with our bare feet symbolizes our grounding to the earth, our connection with nature, and our alignment with the divine energy.

From a scientific perspective, going barefoot has its own set of health benefits. When we walk barefoot, we make direct contact with the ground, and this contact can have a profound impact on our physical and mental well-being. This practice, known as *earthing* or *grounding*, is believed to help balance the body's energy. The earth has a negative charge, and when we make contact with it, our body absorbs electrons, which can help neutralize free radicals and reduce inflammation. This process is thought to reduce stress, improve sleep, and even enhance immune function. In a temple, where people come to seek peace and spiritual connection, going barefoot can help them feel more relaxed, centered, and in harmony with themselves.

Another scientific explanation lies in the idea of acupressure and reflexology. Our feet contain numerous nerve endings that correspond to different parts of the body, and the soles of our feet are thought to be rich with reflex points that can influence our physical and emotional state. Walking barefoot on a surface, especially a natural one like stone or grass, stimulates these reflex points and helps balance the body's energy. In a temple setting, this stimulation can enhance the feeling of well-being, making the experience of worship more immersive and impactful.

Moreover, in many ancient cultures, the temple was not just a place of religious worship but also a center for healing and rejuvenation. The design of temple structures, including the pathways leading to the sanctum sanctorum, was often intentional. Many temples were constructed in such a way that walking barefoot through them allowed the devotees to absorb energy from the ground and align their body's vibrations with the temple's spiritual frequency. Some temples also have certain types of stone flooring that are believed to have therapeutic qualities when walked on barefoot.

On a deeper level, going barefoot in a temple can be seen as a symbolic gesture of shedding one's material attachments and ego. Our shoes are often a representation of the outside world, where we are constantly moving, striving, and dealing with the complexities of life. By leaving our shoes outside the temple, we symbolically leave behind these worldly concerns and enter the sacred space with an open heart, unburdened by the distractions and burdens of the material world. This act of shedding our external identity and ego aligns us with the divine, helping us experience spiritual purity.

One of the most profound aspects of going barefoot in a temple is the connection to the earth and nature. As we walk barefoot, we become more aware of our senses. The texture of the floor, whether it is warm stone, cool marble, or soft grass, heightens our sensory perception. This mindfulness can help us be more present in the moment, opening us up to the divine presence. In many ways, walking barefoot becomes an act of meditation. It brings us into the now, creating a sense of stillness and mindfulness that enhances our spiritual experience.

As I continued to reflect on the practice of going barefoot, I realized that it is not just a custom or a ritual; it is a practice that connects us to the divine on a deeper level. It is a physical, mental, and spiritual act that brings us closer to the earth, the divine energy, and ourselves. The act of removing our shoes before entering a temple is a reminder to step away from our ego, to be humble, and to reconnect with the world around us.

In the end, going barefoot in a temple is a practice that holds great significance. It is an offering of respect, a way to connect with the earth's energy, a form of healing for the body and mind, and a reminder of our spiritual essence. The next time I step into a temple and take off my shoes, I will remember that I am not just following a custom, but participating in a practice that has been passed down through generations—one that connects me to the earth, to the divine, and to my truest self.

Chapter 10:
The Significance of the Mangalsutra

Growing up in a traditional family, I always noticed my mother and aunts wearing the mangalsutra, an essential piece of jewelry that marked the sanctity of marriage. It seemed like an unspoken rule. Every married woman wore it without fail. For the longest time, I never questioned why the mangalsutra was so important or why it had to be worn at all times. It was simply a part of the ritual of marriage, a visible symbol of a woman's married status. But as I entered adulthood and became more curious about traditions and their deeper meanings, I began to question the significance of this ancient custom.

I remember asking my mother one day, "Why is the mangalsutra so important? Why do married women have to wear it all the time? Is it just for show, or does it serve a deeper purpose?" My mother smiled gently and replied, "It's not just for show, my dear. It holds a much deeper meaning." She didn't go into further detail, which left me thinking about it even more.

The more I pondered, the more I became intrigued by the concept. What was the real significance behind the design of the mangalsutra? Why were its elements so carefully chosen? Was there a deeper science that had been passed down through generations?

Over time, I realized that the mangalsutra wasn't just a piece of jewelry but a powerful symbol with profound meaning—one that embodied the essence of marriage and the spiritual bond shared between a husband and wife.

The Design and Its Significance

The mangalsutra is typically made of black beads, gold, and a pendant, and it is worn around the neck of the wife. The black beads, often strung together in a specific pattern, play a key role in safeguarding the marriage. The most common belief is that the black color wards off evil spirits and negative energies, protecting the couple from misfortune. As I researched more, I discovered that the black beads are not just symbolic but also have a scientific basis.

Black, in many cultures, is believed to absorb negative energy. The black beads in a mangalsutra are thought to act as a shield, protecting the wearer from external harm and emotional stress. When you wear a mangalsutra, it acts as a constant reminder of the marriage, creating a positive aura that surrounds you. It's a symbolic safeguard to preserve the harmony in the relationship, and it also represents the strength and durability of the marital bond.

The gold element in the mangalsutra, especially the pendant, is significant as well. Gold is a precious and eternal metal that has been valued across cultures for centuries. Its inclusion in the mangalsutra is symbolic of the purity and strength of the marriage bond. Gold represents the wealth and prosperity that the couple is meant to share together, not just material wealth, but also emotional and spiritual richness.

The design of the mangalsutra often features a pendant, usually shaped like a simple geometrical design or symbol, such as a "V" or a "tulsi" leaf. These designs aren't just decorative; they carry deep symbolic meanings. The "V" shape, for example, represents the union of the two souls in marriage, a symbol of the woman and man coming together in a harmonious relationship. It signifies the balancing of energies between the couple. The tulsi leaf or any other symbolic design often represents purity, longevity, and fertility, which are all essential elements in a successful marriage.

The Role of the Mangalsutra in the Physical and Emotional Connection

As I dug deeper into the symbolism, I also discovered that the mangalsutra has a more scientific basis than I had ever imagined. The necklace sits close to the chest, near the heart, which is the center of emotional and spiritual energy in the body. The close proximity of the mangalsutra to the heart helps maintain an emotional connection between the married couple. The act of wearing it daily serves as a constant reminder of the commitment, responsibilities, and emotional ties that come with marriage.

Moreover, the position of the mangalsutra has an impact on the body's energy system. The black beads and the gold pendant are said to resonate with the body's own electromagnetic field, creating an energy that fosters emotional stability, mental peace, and a sense of well-being. The constant contact with the skin amplifies this energy, providing a grounding effect that can help in overcoming daily stress and anxiety.

A Spiritual Reminder of Commitment

As I delved further into the practice, I realized that the mangalsutra also plays a deeply spiritual role. In many cultures, marriage is not just seen as a legal contract but as a sacred bond, one that involves both the body and soul. The mangalsutra is a physical representation of that bond. By wearing it, a woman is reminded of her commitment to her partner, and vice versa. It symbolizes loyalty, love, and protection, all key aspects that strengthen the marital relationship. It also symbolizes the duty to nurture and protect the bond of marriage, just as the black beads shield the wearer from negative forces.

The ritual of tying the mangalsutra, typically performed by the husband during the wedding ceremony, is a sacred moment. It marks the beginning of a journey together and signifies that the two individuals are now intertwined in a spiritual and emotional partnership. Wearing the mangalsutra thereafter serves as a reminder of this momentous occasion and the responsibilities that come with it.

The Science Behind Wearing the Mangalsutra

One of the most eye-opening aspects for me was understanding the science behind wearing the mangalsutra. It turns out that the materials used in the mangalsutra—gold and black beads—are not chosen at random. The practice of wearing gold has been linked to positive health effects in traditional medicine. Gold is known to have healing properties, and it is believed that wearing gold can help balance the body's energy and improve overall health.

The black beads, on the other hand, are not just decorative but serve a more practical purpose. Black beads are thought to absorb negative energy, preventing the flow of harmful influences. In addition, the weight and pressure of the mangalsutra against the chest create a subtle but effective acupressure on the wearer's heart center, which is said to have calming and grounding effects on the nervous system.

As I learned more, it became clear to me that the mangalsutra was not just a piece of jewelry but a powerful tool that had both emotional and physical benefits. It was a symbol of love, commitment, protection, and spiritual connection, and it carried with it a scientific rationale that made sense on multiple levels.

Now, whenever I wear my mangalsutra, I don't just see it as a piece of jewellery. It has become a meaningful part of my life, reminding me of my bond with my partner and the shared responsibilities that come with it. The mangalsutra is not just a cultural tradition—it is a symbol of love, protection, and the beautiful journey of marriage, one that connects us spiritually, emotionally, and physically.

The design of the **two beads** in a mangalsutra holds significant symbolism, and it varies in its interpretations based on cultural and regional variations. However, the core meaning behind the two beads is consistent across many traditions: it represents the union between the husband and wife, the balance of energies, and the harmony in the marital relationship.

1. Symbol of the Union of Two Souls

One of the most prominent interpretations of the two beads is that they represent the **husband and wife**—two individuals coming together to form a single, unified whole. The two beads symbolize the couple's individual identities that merge into one cohesive bond through marriage. Each bead represents one person, and together they signify the emotional and spiritual union that marriage represents.

- **Husband and Wife**: Just as the two beads are placed together on the mangalsutra, the husband and wife are bound together in the sacred bond of marriage. The beads represent the love, loyalty, and connection between the two individuals, who are now united in a lifelong relationship.

2. The Balance of Energies

In many spiritual traditions, there is a belief that the energies of the masculine and feminine forces must be balanced for harmony in life. The two beads in a mangalsutra symbolize this **balance of energies** between the husband (masculine energy) and wife (feminine energy).

- **Masculine and Feminine Energies**: The beads reflect the complementary relationship between the two energies. The husband and wife play different yet equally important roles in marriage, just as the two beads are distinct yet connected. The balance of these energies is crucial for the harmony and well-being of the couple and their family.

3. The Promise of Protection and Unity

The two beads are often considered to represent the **protective nature of marriage**. The mangalsutra itself, with its black beads, is traditionally worn to ward off negative influences, evil eyes, or any external harm. The two beads, when placed together, enhance the protective power of the mangalsutra.

- **Protection for the Couple**: The two beads can symbolize the shared responsibility of protecting and nurturing each other within the marriage. They act as a reminder of the vows taken to support one another and shield the relationship from external pressures or negativity.

4. Symbol of Fertility and Prosperity

In some regions, the two beads represent the couple's journey to creating a family. **Fertility** and the hope for children are deeply woven into the symbolism of the mangalsutra. In this context, the two beads may signify the unity needed to produce and nurture life, and they serve as a reminder of the divine blessings that come with a committed union.

- **Hope for Children**: The connection between the two beads symbolizes the potential for the couple to grow together, share in the creation of a family, and pass on their values, love, and tradition.

5. Traditional and Spiritual Significance

Beyond the symbolic meanings, the two beads also have **spiritual significance** in certain regions. Some traditions believe that wearing two beads, especially made of specific materials like black or gold, aligns with spiritual practices meant to attract positive energy and blessings.

- **Spiritual Bond**: The two beads can represent the sacred vows taken in marriage, which are not just social but also spiritual. The act of wearing these beads is said to invoke blessings from divine sources, ensuring that the couple remains in harmony with each other and with the higher powers.

6. Aesthetic Balance in the Design

The two beads in the mangalsutra also serve an **aesthetic** purpose, ensuring that the design remains balanced and symmetrical. Whether the beads are identical or of different shapes or sizes, they contribute to the overall harmony of the jewelry, just as a marriage requires balance between the partners.

- **Visual Balance**: The placement of the beads creates a visual equilibrium, which reflects the importance of both partners playing equal and harmonious roles in the marriage. This symmetry in design represents the equilibrium that should exist in the relationship.

In conclusion, the two beads in the mangalsutra are not just ornamental. They hold deep meanings related to the spiritual and emotional bond between a husband and wife. Whether symbolizing the union of two souls, balancing energies, or ensuring protection, these beads are an essential part of the mangalsutra, reminding the wearer of the sacredness, responsibilities, and blessings of marriage.

Chapter 11:
The Science Behind Wearing Gold in the Upper Part of the Body and Silver in the Lower Part of the Body

In traditional Indian culture, the significance of wearing gold and silver jewelry is not just limited to aesthetics or ornamentation, but it is deeply rooted in ancient wisdom, spiritual practices, and scientific principles. One such intriguing custom is the belief in wearing **gold** on the **upper part** of the body, such as on the neck, arms, and fingers, and wearing **silver** on the **lower part** of the body, including the feet and legs. At first glance, these practices may seem purely ornamental, but they are actually backed by science and ancient healing traditions that focus on energy balance, health, and well-being.

The Role of Gold in the Upper Body

Gold has been revered for centuries for its purity, rarity, and aesthetic appeal. Its unique properties also contribute to its special place in the upper part of the body. Here's why gold is traditionally worn in areas like the neck, chest, and hands:

1. Positive Energy and the Heart Chakra

In **Vedic traditions**, the human body is believed to have multiple energy centers known as chakras. The **heart chakra**, located in the center of the chest, is associated with love, compassion, and balance. Gold is thought to have a special connection with this chakra due to its electromagnetic properties. When worn around the upper body, especially near the chest or throat, gold is believed to enhance the flow of positive energy to the heart chakra, promoting emotional and mental well-being.

- **Energy Flow**: Gold has the ability to amplify the energy of love, compassion, and peace, creating a harmonious environment around the wearer. This is why it is considered ideal for the upper body, which houses some of the most vital energy centers in the body, such as the heart and throat.

2. Regulation of Body Temperature

Gold is an excellent conductor of heat, which means it can help regulate the body's temperature when worn on the upper body. The heart, being the center of circulation, needs to maintain a balance of heat and circulation to function efficiently. Gold's ability to absorb and distribute warmth is thought to help maintain this equilibrium, keeping the upper body in a state of balance.

3. Emotional Stability

Gold is considered a metal of **calmness** and **emotional stability**. Wearing gold jewelry on the upper body, particularly near the head and chest, is believed to help alleviate stress and anxiety. It is thought to have a soothing effect, promoting tranquility and clarity in thoughts. This is why many cultures use gold for spiritual practices, as it is believed to bring about peace and positivity.

4. Electromagnetic Properties and the Brain

Gold is also known for its **electromagnetic properties**. It is believed that wearing gold near the brain (in the form of earrings, headpieces, or pendants) can have a positive effect on mental clarity, sharpness, and focus. The electromagnetic interaction between gold and the body is thought to balance the brain's energy, reducing the effects of mental fatigue and stress.

The Role of Silver in the Lower Body

Silver, on the other hand, is typically worn on the **lower part** of the body, such as on the feet, ankles, and legs. It is believed that silver possesses unique properties that complement the energy systems of the lower body. Here's how silver works in the lower part of the body:

1. Cooling Properties

Unlike gold, silver is known for its **cooling properties**. The lower part of the body, especially the legs and feet, is more prone to physical strain and fatigue, as it bears the body's weight. Wearing silver on the lower part of the body is believed to help reduce heat buildup and prevent discomfort. Silver jewelry like anklets or toe rings helps in maintaining a cooling effect, especially in hot climates or after prolonged physical activity.

- **Cooling Effect on Feet**: The feet are known to have a significant number of nerve endings and play an essential role in maintaining the body's balance and circulation. Wearing silver on the feet, therefore, is thought to help reduce inflammation, prevent swelling, and promote overall comfort.

2. Connection to the Root Chakra

The **root chakra** is located at the base of the spine and is believed to be responsible for grounding and stability. Silver, with its reflective and cooling qualities, is thought to support this chakra, helping to keep the wearer grounded and secure. Wearing silver jewelry on the feet or lower part of the body is believed to help the wearer stay in touch with the earth, promoting stability and emotional grounding.

- **Grounding and Stability**: Silver's reflective properties are said to reflect and disperse negative energy, while its grounding nature helps in connecting with the earth. This is particularly important for physical health and emotional stability, as the lower body is the foundation of our overall balance and well-being.

3. Detoxification and Healing Properties

Silver is known for its **purifying and detoxifying properties**. It is believed to have the ability to remove toxins from the body and improve overall circulation. Wearing silver jewelry on the lower part of the body, especially the feet, helps improve the flow of blood and energy throughout the legs, which can reduce pain, improve circulation, and aid in detoxification.

- **Detoxification**: Silver is thought to play a role in detoxifying the body by drawing out impurities and promoting proper metabolic function. This is particularly beneficial for the legs and feet, which can accumulate toxins from daily activities, such as walking or standing.

The Science of Wearing Gold in the Upper Body and Silver in the Lower Body

The practice of wearing gold in the upper part of the body and silver in the lower part of the body aligns with **principles of energy balance** that are found in both traditional and modern sciences. The upper body, with its vital organs, energy centers, and chakras, benefits from the positive, amplifying properties of gold, which help enhance mental clarity, emotional stability, and spiritual well-being. The lower body, on the other hand, is better suited to the cooling, grounding, and purifying effects of silver, which supports circulation, detoxification, and emotional balance.

The Balance of Yin and Yang

In both **Chinese medicine** and **Indian philosophy**, the concepts of **Yin and Yang** or **Prakriti and Purusha** emphasize balance between opposing forces. Gold and silver, when worn on the body in this specific manner, help maintain a balance between these forces. Gold represents the more active, Yang energy (masculine, positive, and expansive), while silver corresponds to Yin energy (feminine, passive, and cooling). By wearing gold on the upper body and silver on the lower body, we are maintaining a harmonious balance of these energies, promoting physical, emotional, and spiritual health.

Conclusion

The tradition of wearing **gold** in the upper part of the body and **silver** in the lower part is not just a cultural norm but a practice rooted in science, energy balance, and holistic well-being. Gold's ability to enhance energy flow, stabilize emotions, and promote mental clarity makes it ideal for the upper body, while silver's cooling, grounding, and detoxifying properties make it the perfect choice for the lower body. Together, they create a balanced energy system that supports both physical and emotional health, making these ancient practices more than just symbolic—they are grounded in science, too.

Chapter 12:
The Science Behind Women Wearing Raksha Sutra in Left Hand and Men in Right Hand

The **Raksha Sutra**, often referred to as the **protective thread** or **sacred thread**, is a significant part of various cultural and spiritual practices, especially in India. It is tied around the wrist to symbolize protection, security, and the invocation of divine blessings. While the practice is commonly associated with the festival of **Raksha Bandhan**, where sisters tie a Rakhi (a form of Raksha Sutra) on their brothers' wrists, it also holds deeper spiritual, scientific, and cultural significance.

One of the notable traditions is that **women wear the Raksha Sutra on their left hand**, and **men wear it on their right hand**. This simple yet powerful custom is deeply rooted in both spiritual and scientific reasoning.

The Significance of the Left and Right Hands in Spiritual and Scientific Terms

Before delving into the specifics of the Raksha Sutra, it's essential to understand why the left and right hands are given distinct roles in traditional practices.

1. Left Hand: Feminine Energy and the Heart Chakra

In many ancient traditions, the **left side** of the body is associated with feminine energy and the **heart chakra**, which governs emotional well-being, love, and relationships. The left side of the body is often linked to the **receptive** and **passive** aspects of an individual's nature, while the right side represents the **active**, **assertive**, and **masculine** aspects.

- **The Left Hand as the Feminine Symbol**: It is believed that the left hand holds the **receptive energy**, making it more attuned to emotions and spiritual connection. By wearing the Raksha Sutra on the left wrist, the woman symbolically connects herself to **protection** and **nurturing** energy, which is traditionally considered to come from the divine, family, or a brother. The protective thread tied to the left hand helps channel this feminine energy toward safeguarding her emotional and spiritual well-being.

2. Right Hand: Masculine Energy and the Solar Plexus Chakra

In contrast, the **right side** of the body is traditionally associated with masculine energy and the **solar plexus chakra**, which is linked to power, will, and action. The right hand is considered to be more **dominant**, **active**, and **projective**.

- **The Right Hand as the Masculine Symbol**: For men, wearing the Raksha Sutra on the right hand is symbolic of their **active role in protecting** and providing security. The right hand, being stronger and more aligned with the masculine energy of action, is the appropriate vessel for receiving protection, as it is believed to resonate with qualities of strength, support, and responsibility. The Raksha Sutra tied on the right hand represents the bond of protection that the man promises to offer, not just to his sister but also to the women in his life.

The Energetic Flow and Chakras

The concept of energy flow in the body, particularly through the **meridian points** and **chakras**, is also a key factor in understanding the significance of wearing the Raksha Sutra on different hands.

1. Energy Flow in the Left Hand

The left hand is believed to correspond with the **moon energy** and the **feminine principle**. It is the side that receives energy from the external world. In this sense, when the Raksha Sutra is tied on the left wrist, it creates a **protective shield** that nurtures and shields the wearer from negative energy while simultaneously **receiving divine blessings**.

- **The Left Hand's Connection to the Heart Chakra**: Since the heart chakra is located near the chest, on the left side of the body, it governs emotions and compassion. The energy from the Raksha Sutra, when tied on the left hand, is believed to circulate through the heart chakra, bringing in **love, peace, and emotional stability**. It creates a strong, harmonious connection between the person and their environment, helping to maintain emotional and spiritual balance.

2. Energy Flow in the Right Hand

The right hand is believed to correspond with the **sun energy** and the **masculine principle**. It is the side that projects outward, expressing willpower and strength. Tying the Raksha Sutra on the right hand helps to channel the wearer's ability to **protect, act, and manifest** their intentions into the world.

- **The Right Hand's Connection to the Solar Plexus Chakra**: The solar plexus chakra, located above the navel, governs personal power, confidence, and decision-making. When the Raksha Sutra is tied to the right hand, it resonates with this chakra, symbolizing the **strength** to protect and the **willpower** to ensure safety for the ones we love. For men, this placement is particularly important as it emphasizes their protective role in their relationships.

The Symbolism of the Raksha Sutra

In Hindu tradition, the **Raksha Sutra** or Rakhi is a sacred thread tied by a sister on her brother's wrist to symbolize the promise of protection. It is believed that when the sister ties the thread, she invokes the **divine protection** of Lord Vishnu, Lord Shiva, or other deities, asking for the well-being and security of her brother.

- **For Women**: Wearing the Raksha Sutra on the left wrist signifies that the woman is the recipient of divine blessings and protection. It's a gesture that not only symbolizes protection from her brother but also aligns her with the cosmic energies of the universe. This tradition emphasizes the woman's role in preserving familial bonds and maintaining emotional equilibrium.

- **For Men**: Wearing the Raksha Sutra on the right wrist signifies the man's role as the protector. It's a promise to safeguard the women and the family, symbolizing **duty, responsibility**, and the **strength of character** that comes with protecting those we care about. The right hand is associated with **action**, and by wearing the Raksha Sutra here, a man aligns himself with his spiritual and familial responsibility.

The Scientific Perspective: Acupressure and Meridian Theory

From a scientific point of view, both the left and right hands are connected to important **meridian points** in **traditional Chinese medicine** (TCM) and **Ayurveda**. The left and right hands have specific pressure points that influence the flow of **energy (Prana or Chi)** in the body.

- **Left Hand**: The left hand is said to be linked to the **yin energy**, which is passive and receptive. By wearing the Raksha Sutra on the left, it is believed to enhance the flow of this receptive energy into the body, creating a calm and nurturing environment for the individual.

- **Right Hand**: The right hand is connected to the **yang energy**, which is active and dynamic. Wearing the Raksha Sutra on the right helps activate this energy, improving the wearer's strength, vigor, and assertiveness, particularly in carrying out protective duties.

Conclusion: The Divine and Practical Significance of Raksha Sutra Placement

The tradition of tying the Raksha Sutra on different wrists for men and women is a symbolic representation of the balance between feminine and masculine energies, with each gender assuming a distinct role in the circle of protection, support, and love. Women wearing the Raksha Sutra on their left hand connect with the **nurturing, protective** energy of the divine, while men wearing it on their right hand take on the **active role of protection** and **strength**.

This practice not only promotes emotional and spiritual well-being but also aligns with deeper scientific principles that govern energy flow, chakras, and meridian points. Thus, the custom of wearing the Raksha Sutra on the left hand for women and the right hand for men beautifully bridges both the spiritual and scientific realms, creating a holistic sense of protection, connection, and balance.

Chapter 13:
The Relation Between the Moon Cycle and Menstruation

The relationship between the **moon cycle** and **menstruation** has been a subject of fascination for centuries. Many ancient cultures, including Indian, Greek, and Egyptian civilizations, observed and documented a connection between the phases of the moon and the female menstrual cycle. This chapter delves into the scientific, spiritual, and cultural perspectives surrounding this connection, explaining why menstruation is often linked to the moon cycle.

The Moon Cycle and the Menstrual Cycle

The **moon cycle**, also known as the **lunar cycle**, lasts about 29.5 days, mirroring the **average length of a woman's menstrual cycle**, which typically ranges from 28 to 30 days. The moon's phases – from new moon to full moon and back – occur over a similar period, leading many to draw correlations between the two. This connection is not only a coincidence but also a reflection of the rhythms and cycles found in nature.

1. Phases of the Moon

The moon goes through different phases during its cycle:

- **New Moon**: The beginning of the lunar cycle, when the moon is not visible from Earth.

- **Waxing Crescent**: The phase when the moon starts to show a sliver of light.

- **First Quarter**: The moon appears as half-lit.

- **Full Moon**: The phase when the entire moon is illuminated and visible.

- **Waning Gibbous**: The moon begins to shrink in size after the full moon.
- **Last Quarter**: Another half-lit phase before the moon disappears into the new moon.

Similarly, the **menstrual cycle** can be divided into different phases:

- **Menstrual Phase**: When bleeding occurs, typically lasting from 3 to 7 days.
- **Follicular Phase**: The phase that starts after menstruation and lasts until ovulation, during which eggs mature in the ovaries.
- **Ovulation**: The release of a matured egg from the ovary.
- **Luteal Phase**: The phase that begins after ovulation and lasts until menstruation starts again.

2. Scientific Explanation

In scientific terms, the **lunar cycle** and the **menstrual cycle** both follow rhythmic patterns. Though there's no conclusive evidence proving a direct connection, several theories suggest that:

- **The Moon's Gravitational Pull**: The gravitational force exerted by the moon is believed to influence water on Earth, including the water within the human body. Since the human body is largely composed of water (about 60-70%), it is speculated that the moon's gravity might have an effect on bodily functions, including menstruation. Some studies have suggested that menstruation could be more likely to occur around the full moon due to the increased gravitational pull.
- **Light Sensitivity and Hormones**: The moon's light has also been theorized to influence hormone production in the human body. The increase in light during the full moon may trigger certain hormonal shifts, which in turn could affect the timing of menstruation. For centuries, women in ancient

cultures would synchronize their menstrual cycles with the lunar phases, potentially due to the influence of moonlight on hormonal balance.

- **Biological Rhythm**: Both the menstrual cycle and the lunar cycle are biological rhythms, and the synchronization between the two may be due to the body's natural tendency to align itself with environmental and cosmic patterns. The idea of circadian rhythms, which regulate the body's natural sleep-wake cycle, may extend to other biological cycles as well, including menstruation.

3. Historical and Cultural Significance

In various cultures, the moon has long been associated with femininity, fertility, and the menstrual cycle. The phases of the moon were often seen as a reflection of the feminine experience – waxing and waning, fluctuating between fullness and emptiness, much like the menstrual cycle. Let's explore some of the cultural beliefs:

- **Hinduism**: In Hindu tradition, the moon is often linked with the goddess **Chandralekha** or **Soma**, who is associated with the feminine energies of the universe. The menstrual cycle is considered sacred, and many spiritual practices align with the phases of the moon. Some believe that menstruation during the full moon is particularly powerful, as the full moon is a time of energy culmination and divine connection.

- **Ancient Greece**: In ancient Greece, the goddess **Artemis** was the moon goddess and the protector of women's health, especially during their reproductive years. The Greeks believed that the moon and menstrual cycles were intrinsically linked, and women would often celebrate the full moon as a symbol of fertility and womanhood.

- **Native American Cultures**: Many Native American tribes also recognized the connection between the moon and menstruation. They referred to the menstrual cycle as the

moon time and saw it as a sacred and powerful event that aligned with the cycles of nature. Women would often retreat to a special place to honor this sacred time, connecting with their inner wisdom and the energies of the earth and moon.

- **Chinese Traditions**: In Chinese medicine, the moon is associated with **yin energy** (the feminine, passive, and nurturing force). The full moon is said to amplify the yin energy, making it a time of spiritual and emotional renewal, much like the menstrual cycle, which is seen as a time for release and cleansing.

4. The Full Moon and Menstruation

While it is not scientifically proven that menstruation always aligns with the full moon, many women experience their period around the full moon. This phenomenon is more noticeable in traditional societies where women's cycles were less influenced by modern technology, artificial lighting, and medications that regulate menstrual cycles. In these societies, it was common for groups of women to menstruate around the same time, often during the full moon, and this collective experience was considered spiritually significant.

The full moon, in particular, is seen as a time of **culmination and completion**, and some women believe that their menstruation during this phase symbolizes a cleansing and renewal process. Just as the moon reaches its fullest expression during the full moon, women feel the release and culmination of their menstrual cycle, symbolizing the end of one phase and the beginning of another.

Conclusion: Connecting the Moon and Menstruation

The connection between the **moon cycle** and **menstruation** is multifaceted, blending scientific theories with spiritual and cultural beliefs. Whether it's due to the gravitational effects of the moon, the influence of moonlight on hormones, or the body's innate rhythm aligning with cosmic cycles, this relationship has been acknowledged across cultures and societies.

For many women, their menstrual cycle is not just a biological process but a spiritual and sacred experience, deeply intertwined with the cycles of the earth, the moon, and the universe. By understanding this connection, we can appreciate the profound significance of both the moon and menstruation in our lives, recognizing them as vital forces of nature that sustain, renew, and empower us.

Chapter 14:
The Science Behind Wearing a Copper Ring

Wearing a **copper ring** has been a tradition in various cultures and is often associated with health benefits, spiritual practices, and cultural beliefs. In this chapter, we will explore the scientific reasons behind wearing a copper ring, its potential health benefits, and how this ancient practice has withstood the test of time.

The Historical Significance of Copper Rings

Copper has been used by humans for thousands of years for its properties and benefits. Ancient civilizations, including the Egyptians, Greeks, and Indians, used copper for various purposes, including jewelry, utensils, and even as a symbol of health and protection. Copper rings, specifically, have long been associated with:

- **Healing properties**: Ancient cultures believed copper had the power to cure ailments and provide protection from negative energies.

- **Symbolism**: In many cultures, wearing a copper ring was a sign of wisdom, health, and spiritual connection.

- **Tradition**: In some parts of the world, wearing copper jewelry is still a cultural or religious practice, passed down through generations.

The belief in the power of copper is not just based on tradition but has scientific backing in many cases.

The Science of Copper and Its Benefits

Copper is a trace element that plays a crucial role in many biological functions within the human body. It is essential for the formation of red blood cells, absorption of iron, and the maintenance of the nervous system. It also plays a role in the production of collagen, a protein that is vital for the health of connective tissues, skin, and bones. The connection between copper and health explains why it has been used in various forms for health-related purposes.

1. Copper's Effect on the Human Body

When copper rings are worn on the fingers, it is believed that they help in **transferring small amounts of copper** into the body through the skin. This process is thought to help:

- **Improve circulation**: Copper is believed to have properties that help stimulate blood circulation. For those suffering from conditions like arthritis, the wearing of copper rings is said to help alleviate joint pain by increasing blood flow and reducing inflammation.

- **Balance energy**: In holistic health practices, copper is often associated with positive energy flow. It is believed to conduct energy and help balance the body's natural electromagnetic field. Some people believe that wearing copper jewelry helps in channeling this energy through the body, promoting physical and emotional well-being.

- **Joint and muscle relief**: Copper rings are commonly worn by individuals suffering from arthritis or other joint conditions. Copper has anti-inflammatory properties, and the small amount of copper absorbed through the skin is thought to help reduce pain and swelling in the joints.

2. Copper's Antibacterial and Antiviral Properties

Copper has been scientifically shown to have **antimicrobial properties**. It can kill or inhibit the growth of bacteria, viruses, and fungi on its surface. This is one reason why copper is often used in hospital settings for door handles, faucets, and other high-contact surfaces. When copper rings are worn, they may help reduce the buildup of harmful bacteria, especially in areas like the hands, which are frequently exposed to germs.

3. Magnetic Field and Copper Rings

Some proponents of wearing copper jewelry claim that it has a **magnetic effect** that can influence the body's electromagnetic field. The human body has its own electromagnetic field, and it is believed that copper rings can help balance this field. For individuals who feel out of sync with their surroundings, the copper ring is thought to restore harmony by boosting the body's natural energy flow. While scientific evidence supporting the magnetic effects of copper on the human body is limited, many individuals continue to report feeling better when wearing copper jewelry.

The Spiritual and Healing Aspect of Copper Rings

Copper is also valued in **spiritual practices**, particularly in relation to healing and protection. Many people believe that copper has a strong connection with the **root chakra**, which is linked to grounding and stability. When a copper ring is worn on the finger, it is thought to enhance feelings of security, emotional well-being, and balance. For those who practice energy healing, copper rings are often seen as a tool to open and align energy pathways, helping to channel healing energy into the body.

- **Healing energy**: In traditional healing practices, copper is thought to amplify energy, especially when the body is in need of healing. By wearing a copper ring, one may experience a boost in energy levels, which can help in recovery from illness or fatigue.

- **Protection from negative energy**: Copper is often seen as a metal that attracts positive energy while repelling negative influences. It is believed that wearing a copper ring can protect an individual from emotional or spiritual negativity and enhance their sense of inner peace.

The Cultural Significance of Copper Rings

The practice of wearing copper rings is not only rooted in scientific principles but also in **cultural significance**. In various parts of the world, copper rings are seen as symbols of:

- **Strength and protection**: Copper rings are thought to ward off negative influences and offer protection to the wearer. In certain cultures, they are worn as a shield against evil or misfortune.

- **Tradition and family legacy**: In some families, wearing a copper ring is a custom passed down from generation to generation. It is seen as a way of honoring one's ancestors and keeping the family tradition alive.

- **Symbol of wealth and prosperity**: In some cultures, copper is associated with **abundance and prosperity**. The wearing of copper rings can symbolize the desire for material and spiritual wealth.

Conclusion: Understanding the Benefits of Copper Rings

The science behind wearing a **copper ring** blends both **physical health benefits** and **spiritual significance**. While scientific studies have shown that copper may aid in circulation, joint pain relief, and energy balance, the spiritual and cultural aspects of wearing copper are equally important to many people. Whether it is the antimicrobial properties, the magnetic effects, or the healing energy associated with copper, the significance of wearing a copper ring continues to resonate with individuals seeking both physical and emotional well-being.

In the modern world, where many people look for natural solutions to health problems, wearing a copper ring may offer both practical and symbolic benefits. For those who believe in its power, the copper ring serves not only as an accessory but as a tool for healing, balance, and protection—an ancient practice that continues to endure in today's society.

Chapter 15:
Water and Energy: The Transformative Influence of External Forces on Molecular Structure

There have been various experiments carried out to show how water molecules change their structure based on the energy or influences they are exposed to. These experiments suggest that water has a unique ability to adapt its molecular structure in response to external stimuli such as thoughts, emotions, sound, and environmental factors. Here are a few notable experiments that have explored this phenomenon:

1. Dr. Masaru Emoto's Water Crystals Experiment

Dr. Masaru Emoto, a Japanese researcher, is one of the most well-known figures in studies of how water responds to energy and human consciousness. His experiment demonstrated that water can change its molecular structure depending on the type of energy it is exposed to.

Experiment Details:

- **Water exposed to positive influences**: Dr. Emoto exposed water to positive emotions, words, music, and prayers. When the water was frozen, the ice crystals formed beautiful, symmetrical, and harmonious patterns, indicating that positive energy had an influence on the molecular structure of the water.

- **Water exposed to negative influences**: On the other hand, when water was exposed to negative emotions, words, or harsh sounds, the resulting crystals were fragmented, irregular, and asymmetrical, suggesting that negative energy had disrupted the structure of the water.

Conclusion:

Dr. Emoto's experiment suggested that the molecular structure of water could be influenced by the energy around it, and that thoughts, words, and emotions could impact the shape of water crystals. His work supported the idea that water has memory and can respond to external stimuli.

2. The Impact of Sound on Water: The Cymatics Experiment

Cymatics is the study of visible sound and vibration patterns, and it has been used to show how sound waves can influence the structure of water.

Experiment Details:

- **Sound frequencies and water**: In cymatic experiments, sound waves are played through water (or water-based substances like sand on a plate). The sound vibrations cause the water (or the sand) to form specific geometric patterns.

- **Music and vibrations**: Water exposed to different types of music also exhibited varying patterns. Classical music, for example, produced symmetrical, calming shapes, while aggressive or dissonant sounds resulted in chaotic and irregular forms.

Conclusion:

The cymatics experiments revealed that sound vibrations significantly affect the structure of water, with different frequencies creating distinct patterns. This experiment highlights the connection between energy (in the form of sound) and the molecular arrangement of water.

3. Emotional Influence on Water: The Influence of Intentions

Several experiments have been conducted to explore how the intentions or emotions of people influence water, particularly its molecular arrangement.

Experiment Details:

- **Intention-based water studies**: In these experiments, individuals would focus their thoughts and intentions on water before freezing it. Positive thoughts and intentions (like love or gratitude) were said to result in the formation of beautiful, symmetrical crystals, while negative thoughts (such as anger or hatred) led to chaotic or broken crystal patterns.
- **Group influence**: Some studies involved groups of people, with one group focusing positive thoughts and another focusing negative thoughts on water samples. Similar to the individual-focused studies, the group that focused on positive intentions saw beautiful crystals form, while the negative group resulted in distorted or incomplete crystals.

Conclusion:

These experiments support the idea that water's molecular structure is highly sensitive to human emotions and intentions. It suggests that water can react to the energy fields surrounding it, including human consciousness and collective intention.

4. The Effect of Words on Water: "Thank You" vs. "I Hate You" Experiment

Building on Dr. Masaru Emoto's work, other studies focused on how written words or phrases could alter water's molecular structure.

Experiment Details:

- **Water with written words**: In these experiments, water containers were labeled with different words, such as "love," "thank you," or "I hate you." After a period of time, the water was frozen, and its crystal formation was examined.
- **Positive vs. negative labels**: Similar to Dr. Emoto's findings, containers labeled with words like "love" or "thank

you" showed beautifully formed crystals, while those labeled with negative phrases like "I hate you" exhibited fragmented, irregular, and distorted crystals.

Conclusion:

The experiment demonstrated that written words—imbued with intention or meaning—could influence the molecular structure of water, further supporting the concept that water can respond to the energy of human consciousness.

5. Water and the Influence of Color: Light Frequency and Molecular Change

In certain studies, it has been shown that color, which is essentially light energy, can also impact the structure of water molecules.

Experiment Details:

- **Color and light exposure**: In these experiments, water was exposed to different colors of light, each with its own frequency and vibrational energy. Water's response to these colors was studied by freezing the water and analyzing the crystal patterns formed under a microscope.

- **Vibrational energy of light**: It was found that each color of light produced distinct patterns in the water crystals. For instance, blue light, which is calming, tended to produce more harmonious patterns, while colors like red and yellow (associated with warmth and energy) produced more dynamic and irregular crystal structures.

Conclusion:

This experiment revealed that light frequencies, which correspond to different colors, have the ability to affect the vibrational energy of water. This further strengthens the idea that water is sensitive to various types of energy and can respond by altering its molecular structure.

6. Water and Environmental Influences: Natural vs. Artificial Sources

This type of experiment focuses on how the source and environment of the water affect its energy and structure.

Experiment Details:

- **Natural vs. tap water**: Natural spring water, collected from pristine environments, has been shown to have more symmetrical, well-structured molecular formations when compared to tap water. The latter is often subjected to chemicals like chlorine and fluoride, which may disrupt its molecular structure.

- **Geopathic stress and water**: Water in environments with geopathic stress (areas where Earth's magnetic fields are disturbed) has been shown to exhibit distorted molecular patterns compared to water from naturally balanced environments.

Conclusion:

Water's structure is influenced by its source and environment. Clean, natural water exhibits more harmonious molecular structures, while water from artificial sources or those affected by environmental stressors may have more irregular or disturbed structures.

Conclusion:

These experiments collectively highlight the incredible sensitivity of water to external energy influences, including sound, thoughts, words, light, and environmental factors. Water, as a molecule, appears to have the ability to change its structure based on the energy it encounters, which can be seen as supporting the idea that water is not only a vital physical substance but also a medium through which energy can be transferred and stored. The research into how water molecules respond to energy is still ongoing, but these experiments lay the foundation for understanding water's remarkable connection to consciousness and the universe.

Chapter 16:
The Science Behind Sleeping Direction

In many ancient cultures and spiritual practices, the direction in which we sleep has always been considered important for health, peace, and prosperity. Vastu Shastra, Feng Shui, and other traditional knowledge systems emphasize sleeping in certain directions to achieve physical, mental, and emotional well-being. In this chapter, we explore the science behind sleeping direction and the potential effects it can have on our body, mind, and overall health.

The Ancient Wisdom of Sleeping Directions

According to Vastu Shastra, an ancient Indian science of architecture and design, the ideal sleeping direction depends on aligning the body with the natural energy forces of the Earth. Vastu suggests that the best directions for sleeping are east, south, or northeast, while sleeping in certain other directions is considered harmful. For example, sleeping with the head facing north is generally advised against in Vastu, as it is believed to interfere with the Earth's magnetic field, leading to disturbed sleep and poor health.

Similarly, in Chinese Feng Shui, the alignment of the bed is linked to the flow of Qi (or Chi), the vital life energy that is believed to flow through everything in the universe. Feng Shui recommends sleeping with the head facing south or east for positive energy and good health.

The Science of the Earth's Magnetic Field

One of the primary reasons behind the advice to sleep in specific directions is the Earth's magnetic field. The Earth acts as a giant magnet with a magnetic north and south pole. Our body also has its own electromagnetic field, and it is believed that when we sleep, the alignment of our body with the Earth's magnetic field can affect the balance and flow of energy in our body.

1. **Head Facing North**: According to both Vastu and modern science, when we sleep with our head facing north, we may inadvertently align our body with the Earth's magnetic field in a way that is not optimal. The Earth's magnetic field flows from the north to the south, and when we lie with our head in the north, it could disrupt the natural flow of blood and energy in our body, leading to restlessness, disturbed sleep, and even potential health problems like headaches, high blood pressure, and increased stress.

2. **Head Facing South**: Sleeping with the head facing south is said to align with the Earth's magnetic field in a way that promotes health and restful sleep. This direction is believed to harmonize the body's energy with the Earth's energy flow, resulting in better circulation, reduced stress, and deeper, more restorative sleep.

3. **Head Facing East**: Sleeping with the head facing east is recommended in many traditions for mental clarity and spiritual well-being. It is believed that the magnetic field of the Earth, in combination with the rising sun in the east, can enhance mental clarity, improve concentration, and stimulate creativity. This direction is also considered favorable for those seeking a peaceful and harmonious sleep experience.

4. **Head Facing West**: Sleeping with the head facing west is often considered less ideal than the other directions. While it is not as harmful as sleeping with the head facing north, it can still lead to disturbed sleep patterns and a sense of imbalance in the body. In Vastu, this direction is linked to the setting sun, which can represent the closing of energy cycles and may not be conducive to restful sleep.

The Role of Melatonin and Circadian Rhythms

One of the scientific explanations for the effects of sleeping direction can also be understood through the lens of melatonin production and circadian rhythms. Our body follows a natural 24-hour cycle called the circadian rhythm, which is influenced by external factors like light, temperature, and magnetic fields. This internal clock regulates sleep, wakefulness, and various bodily functions.

1. **Magnetic Fields and Melatonin**: Research has shown that exposure to magnetic fields can affect the production of melatonin, the hormone responsible for regulating sleep. Sleeping in a direction that disrupts the Earth's magnetic field could potentially affect melatonin production and disturb the body's natural sleep-wake cycle, leading to poor sleep quality and related health issues.

2. **The Role of the Sun's Energy**: In the morning, the sun's energy plays a key role in signaling the body to wake up, and the body's circadian rhythm is calibrated to this natural light cycle. Sleeping with the head facing east, where the sun rises, is thought to help synchronize the body's internal clock with the Earth's energy cycle, promoting better sleep quality and a more balanced rhythm throughout the day.

Psychological and Emotional Impact of Sleeping Direction

In addition to the physical effects of sleeping direction, there may also be psychological and emotional factors at play. Sleeping in a direction that aligns with natural energy forces can bring a sense of calm, balance, and peace, while misalignment with these forces can lead to feelings of unease, anxiety, and restlessness.

For example, many people find that they sleep more soundly when they follow traditional recommendations for sleeping directions. Others report feeling more energized and focused after sleeping with their head facing the right direction. On the other hand, individuals who sleep with their head facing north or west may feel more irritable, stressed, or disconnected from their surroundings.

Modern Scientific Perspective on Sleeping Directions

While the traditional beliefs around sleeping directions may sound unscientific to some, recent studies on electromagnetic fields and their impact on the human body are starting to shed light on the potential effects of sleeping direction. Research into the body's response to magnetic fields, as well as studies on the circadian rhythm and sleep quality, suggests that there may be more to the traditional wisdom than meets the eye.

While it is difficult to scientifically prove that sleeping with the head facing a particular direction has a universal effect on health, many people who practice traditional sleeping habits report positive outcomes in terms of both physical and mental well-being. This could be due to a combination of factors, including the alignment of the body with natural magnetic forces, the influence of sunlight, and the psychological benefits of following a routine that is rooted in ancient wisdom.

Conclusion

The science behind sleeping direction ties together ancient wisdom with modern scientific research on the Earth's magnetic field, circadian rhythms, and the impact of environmental factors on our health. While sleeping direction may not be a magic solution for all health issues, it is worth considering the potential benefits of aligning our body with the natural energy forces of the Earth. By doing so, we can improve the quality of our sleep, enhance our physical health, and experience greater emotional well-being.

Chapter 17:
The Science Behind Janayu Sanskar

Janayu Sanskar, also known as the sacred thread ceremony or Upanayana, is a significant ritual in Hindu culture, particularly among Brahmins, Kshatriyas, and Vaishyas. It marks the initiation of a young boy into formal education and is a rite of passage that signifies the beginning of his journey toward spiritual growth and intellectual development. The ceremony involves the wearing of a sacred thread, called the *janayu* (also known as *yajnopavita*), which is typically worn across the chest and under the shoulder. While this ritual has deep spiritual and cultural significance, in this chapter, we will explore the scientific aspects behind Janayu Sanskar and its impact on the wearer.

The Cultural Significance of Janayu Sanskar

The Janayu Sanskar is considered an important rite of passage in Hinduism, usually performed when a boy reaches the age of 7 or 8. During this ceremony, the boy is given a sacred thread, which is said to symbolize his entry into a higher state of spiritual awareness. The ritual often involves the recitation of mantras, performing prayers, and receiving blessings from elders and spiritual guides. The sacred thread is typically made of three strands, symbolizing the unity of *Brahma* (the creator), *Vishnu* (the preserver), and *Shiva* (the destroyer), and is worn as a reminder of the wearer's connection to the divine.

The *janayu* is not merely a religious symbol; it is also thought to serve as a reminder of the wearer's commitment to Dharma (righteousness), and the ceremony marks the transition from childhood to a more responsible stage of life.

The Scientific Significance of Janayu

While the religious and spiritual aspects of Janayu Sanskar are well-known, it is interesting to explore the scientific rationale behind wearing the sacred thread. The following factors help explain the benefits of wearing the *janayu*.

1. **Material and Conductivity**: The *janayu* is traditionally made of cotton or other natural fibers. These materials have specific properties that contribute to the positive impact of the thread on the body. Cotton, for instance, is a highly conductive material, allowing the wearer to remain connected to the Earth's natural energy field. This is consistent with many traditional practices that emphasize the importance of staying grounded to the earth's electromagnetic field.

2. **Acupressure Points and Nerve Stimulation**: The positioning of the *janayu* on the body is also significant. It is worn across the chest and under the left shoulder, where the three strands of the thread touch specific acupressure points. The human body has numerous nerve endings that are sensitive to touch, and the pressure exerted by the *janayu* on these points may stimulate these nerve endings, improving blood circulation and energy flow throughout the body.

The left side of the body, particularly the heart region, is believed to be more closely connected to the emotional and spiritual aspects of a person, which is why the *janayu* is worn on the left shoulder. The physical pressure from the sacred thread may help in balancing the energy flow, aligning the body and mind, and promoting emotional well-being.

3. **Electromagnetic Field and Chakra Activation**: The human body is an energetic system, and it interacts with the electromagnetic field of the Earth. Wearing the *janayu* is believed to help in balancing the body's energy fields, specifically the chakras. In particular, the heart chakra (*Anahata*) and the throat chakra (*Vishuddha*) are said to be aligned with the sacred thread.

The positioning of the thread across the chest and shoulder may serve as a reminder to align the energy centers (chakras), especially the heart chakra, which governs love, compassion, and emotional healing. The thread may also have a stabilizing effect on the wearer's energy, promoting harmony and balance within the body.

4. **Mindfulness and Consciousness**: The act of wearing the *janayu* itself can bring a heightened sense of mindfulness to the wearer. It acts as a constant reminder of one's duties and responsibilities, which is the core idea of Dharma. The sacred thread is meant to remind the wearer to live in a way that is aligned with righteous conduct, truthfulness, and self-discipline.

Studies have shown that physical reminders (like the *janayu*) can have psychological effects, as they prompt the wearer to be more conscious of their actions, thoughts, and emotions. This heightened awareness can contribute to better decision-making, improved self-discipline, and a deeper sense of responsibility toward oneself and others.

5. **Biological Connection to Water and Earth**: In traditional practices, the *janayu* is often dipped in water, and it is believed to be sanctified and energized in the process. Water, being a conductor of energy, carries and transmits vibrations that can influence the wearer's energy field. This ritual may serve to amplify the wearer's connection to the elements of nature—earth, water, air, and fire—which are considered essential to maintaining balance in the body and mind.

In addition, the act of wearing the thread, which is made of natural materials, may help the wearer stay connected to the Earth's magnetic field. This connection is thought to foster an increased sense of stability and grounding, helping the wearer manage stress and anxiety while maintaining a balanced state of mind.

6. **Psychological and Symbolic Impact**: The *janayu* serves as a powerful psychological symbol. Wearing the sacred thread

on a daily basis serves to reinforce the wearer's identity as someone who is committed to learning, personal growth, and spiritual development. The belief that one has crossed a threshold from childhood to adulthood gives the individual a sense of responsibility and purpose.

This psychological effect is consistent with the concept of the "placebo effect," where the wearer's belief in the power of the sacred thread may, in itself, create positive changes in their mindset, behavior, and overall health.

The Legacy of Janayu Sanskar

In modern times, Janayu Sanskar and the wearing of the *janayu* may be seen as a cultural practice that holds both spiritual and scientific significance. The practice continues to be an integral part of Hindu culture, representing the transition into a more disciplined and responsible phase of life. Though the understanding of its benefits may differ between individuals and cultures, the scientific principles underlying the sacred thread ceremony remain relevant even today.

The Janayu Sanskar is not just a ceremonial rite but a holistic practice that connects the physical, mental, emotional, and spiritual dimensions of life. Whether through the stimulation of acupressure points, the balance of the electromagnetic field, or the reinforcement of personal responsibility, the *janayu* serves as a constant reminder of one's connection to the divine and the universe.

In conclusion, the Janayu Sanskar is a profound tradition that bridges the gap between spirituality and science. It exemplifies how ancient rituals can have practical implications on health, well-being, and personal growth. By understanding the science behind the sacred thread and its impact on the body and mind, we can appreciate the deeper layers of this ancient practice and its relevance in modern life.

Chapter 18:
The Significance of Ritu Kala Samskara

Ritu Kala Samskara, also known as the rite of passage for women's menstrual cycle, is an ancient Hindu ritual that acknowledges the physical and spiritual transformation a girl undergoes once she attains puberty. This samskara plays a vital role in a girl's life, marking the beginning of her adulthood and the onset of fertility. It is a key part of Hindu tradition, deeply ingrained in the cultural and spiritual fabric, and is also seen as a time for a girl to embrace the responsibilities and changes in her life with grace.

While the ritual has cultural and religious significance, it is essential to understand the underlying scientific aspects and the role it plays in the holistic development of an individual, particularly a young woman. In this chapter, we will explore the importance of Ritu Kala Samskara from both a cultural and scientific perspective.

The Cultural and Spiritual Significance of Ritu Kala Samskara

In traditional Hindu culture, Ritu Kala Samskara was typically performed once a girl reached puberty, signifying her transition from childhood to womanhood. The ceremony is marked by the first appearance of menstruation, a crucial event in a girl's life, and is treated with reverence and respect.

The ceremony is often conducted by the elders of the family, particularly the mother and grandmother, who guide the young girl through the customs and rituals associated with menstruation. It is also believed to purify the young girl and prepare her for the duties of womanhood.

In ancient Hindu scriptures, the Ritu Kala Samskara was described as a way to honor the menstrual cycle, a natural process of creation and fertility. The menstrual cycle was considered sacred, and menstruation itself was seen as a sign of a woman's ability to create life, connect with the divine, and embody the energy of *Shakti*, the divine feminine energy.

A significant aspect of the ceremony involves the girl's seclusion during her menstruation. During this time, the girl is expected to rest and refrain from participating in certain activities. This period of seclusion was believed to protect the woman's energy and offer a time for introspection, self-care, and spiritual growth.

Though there were various social and cultural beliefs surrounding menstruation, one of the most important elements was that the girl was now eligible to participate in other rituals, such as marriage and motherhood, and take on more responsibilities in the family and society. This ritual marked the onset of her adulthood and a shift in her role within the family.

The Science Behind Ritu Kala Samskara

1. **Biological Transformation and Puberty**: Menstruation marks the biological transformation from a girl to a woman. Puberty brings about hormonal changes, the development of secondary sexual characteristics, and the ability to conceive. The menstrual cycle is an important marker of fertility and plays a critical role in the reproductive health of a woman.

   From a scientific standpoint, the Ritu Kala Samskara acknowledges and celebrates this natural biological event. It gives the girl a sense of importance and responsibility as she transitions into adulthood. Recognizing this process at an early age also contributes to a greater sense of self-awareness and acceptance of one's body.

2. **Physical and Mental Health Benefits of Rest**: One of the key components of the Ritu Kala Samskara was the practice of rest during menstruation. The girl was typically expected

to rest and refrain from participating in physically demanding tasks. While in some cultures this rest may have been viewed as a form of social isolation, there is a deeper scientific reasoning for allowing the body to rest during menstruation.

Menstruation often involves hormonal fluctuations and physical symptoms such as cramps, fatigue, and mood swings. Resting during this time can have a positive impact on the girl's physical and mental well-being. It allows the body to recuperate and restores energy levels, enabling a smoother transition through the menstrual cycle. Adequate rest also minimizes the risk of menstrual-related disorders, such as heavy bleeding or cramps, and supports the proper functioning of the endocrine and reproductive systems.

Moreover, the period of seclusion provides time for mental peace and introspection, which can contribute to a sense of emotional stability. By allowing girls to embrace their menstrual cycle in a calm and reflective space, the ritual of Ritu Kala Samskara fosters mental clarity and emotional balance.

3. **Spiritual Connection and Energy Preservation**: In Hinduism, menstruation is considered sacred, and it is believed that during menstruation, a woman's energy is at its peak. The Ritu Kala Samskara ritual, which involves a period of seclusion and reflection, is meant to preserve and channel this energy into spiritual growth and personal empowerment.

This idea has roots in the concept of energy balance in the body. Menstruation is a time when the body releases excess energies, and the ritual of resting during this period helps ensure that the energy is not wasted or depleted by unnecessary physical or mental exertion. During the seclusion, the girl is encouraged to focus on inner spiritual practices, such as prayer, meditation, and reflection. These practices allow her to align with the divine energies and develop a stronger connection with her own inner power.

Furthermore, many traditional cultures emphasize that menstrual blood is sacred and represents fertility and creation. By embracing menstruation as a natural and sacred part of life, the ritual encourages a girl to recognize her body's unique abilities and honor her role as a creator, a nurturer, and a woman. This practice of spiritual reverence for menstruation can enhance a woman's sense of self-worth and empowerment.

4. **Fostering Emotional Maturity**: The period of Ritu Kala Samskara is not just a biological transformation, but an emotional one as well. The rituals involved in the ceremony serve to build emotional maturity and strength. A girl, who once may have felt discomfort or embarrassment about menstruation, is now encouraged to accept it as a natural, sacred event.

The guidance from elders, such as the mother and grandmother, helps to provide emotional support and strength during this transition. The girl is empowered to approach the changes in her body with grace, responsibility, and a deeper sense of connection to her lineage and culture.

5. **Creating a Positive Mindset toward Menstruation**: One of the greatest benefits of Ritu Kala Samskara is that it helps foster a positive mindset toward menstruation. In many cultures, menstruation has historically been shrouded in stigma and considered impure or shameful. The Ritu Kala Samskara, however, elevates the status of menstruation as something to be respected and celebrated.

In modern times, this ritual encourages young girls to understand menstruation as a natural and healthy part of life rather than something to be ashamed of. It helps break the taboos surrounding menstruation, contributing to better menstrual hygiene practices and mental health awareness for young women.

The Legacy of Ritu Kala Samskara

Ritu Kala Samskara is an ancient ritual that plays an essential role in a girl's growth and development. It marks an important transition in her life, both biologically and spiritually. In the past, the ritual helped young girls gain a deeper understanding of the changes they were experiencing and allowed them to approach adulthood with maturity and respect for their bodies.

In contemporary society, Ritu Kala Samskara can still hold significant value. Although the practice may not be as widespread, its cultural, biological, and emotional benefits are timeless. By understanding the scientific and spiritual reasons behind this ritual, we can ensure that future generations of women embrace their menstrual cycle as a powerful and transformative experience.

In conclusion, Ritu Kala Samskara is much more than a traditional ritual; it is a holistic practice that supports a girl's physical, mental, and spiritual development. By honoring menstruation and allowing girls to rest, reflect, and reconnect with their inner selves, we create a foundation for healthy, empowered, and self-aware women who carry forward the legacy of this ancient tradition.

Chapter 19:
The Celebration of Menstruation at Kamakhya Devi Temple

The Kamakhya Devi Temple, nestled in the Nilachal Hills of Assam, India, is one of the most revered and ancient Shakti Peethas in Hinduism. It is dedicated to the goddess Kamakhya, who is believed to represent the divine feminine energy, *Shakti*. What makes this temple particularly unique is the extraordinary and sacred tradition it upholds: the celebration of menstruation.

Unlike the societal taboos and restrictions surrounding menstruation in many cultures, the Kamakhya Temple stands as a testament to the reverence and sanctity of the menstrual cycle. The temple's association with menstruation is not just a cultural curiosity, but a profound symbol of feminine power, fertility, and the cyclical nature of life.

In this chapter, we will delve into the celebration of menstruation at Kamakhya Devi Temple, exploring its deep spiritual and cultural significance. We will examine how this sacred tradition connects menstruation with the cosmic rhythm of creation, life, and renewal, offering a unique and empowering perspective on a natural biological event.

The Sacred Menstruation Ritual at Kamakhya

Kamakhya Devi Temple is unique for its association with the goddess's menstruation cycle, which is celebrated annually in a grand and sacred festival. Unlike the usual view of menstruation as impure or unclean, Kamakhya Temple treats menstruation as a divine, sacred phenomenon. It is believed that during this time, the goddess Kamakhya is menstruating, and the temple undergoes a special ritual to honor this cosmic event.

The most significant part of the celebration happens in the month of *Ahaar*, which typically falls in June. This period coincides with the annual Ambubachi Mela, the biggest festival at Kamakhya Temple, during which the goddess Kamakhya is said to be in her menstruation phase. The temple is closed for a few days during this time to allow the goddess to rest and undergo her divine cycle, mirroring the natural menstrual cycle of women.

It is believed that during these days, the temple's sanctum is in a state of 'impurity' or *ashuddhi*, and the goddess's symbolic menstrual blood flows in the form of *Yoni* (a sacred representation of the female genitalia). The goddess's menstruation is revered as a powerful expression of creation and the generative force of life. The temple's closing during this period is seen not as a sign of impurity, but as an important part of maintaining cosmic order and purity.

The festival culminates with a special ceremony marking the end of the menstruation phase, after which the temple is re-opened, and devotees are allowed to enter. This reopening is seen as the re-emergence of the goddess's creative and life-giving energy, signifying a renewal of life, growth, and prosperity.

Symbolism of Menstruation at Kamakhya Temple

At Kamakhya, menstruation is not seen as a sign of impurity, but as an expression of the goddess's powerful, creative energy. This tradition challenges the conventional, negative associations of menstruation, highlighting its importance in the cycle of life. In this context, Kamakhya's menstruation represents the cosmic rhythm of creation, sustenance, and destruction, essential processes in the universal cycle of life.

The symbolism of menstruation at Kamakhya Temple links the physical process of menstruation to the divine, recognizing it as a necessary and powerful force of creation. Just as a woman's menstrual cycle plays a central role in reproduction and the continuity of life, Kamakhya's menstruation is believed to embody the same force—the flow of divine life energy, *Shakti*, that sustains the world.

The *Yoni* worshipped in the temple is a symbolic representation of the goddess's vagina, a natural symbol of fertility, creation, and the cycle of birth and death. The temple's association with menstruation is also indicative of the fertility of the earth, which, like the human body, undergoes cycles of growth, decline, and renewal.

In this spiritual sense, Kamakhya Temple transforms the perception of menstruation. It becomes not an act of "separation" from the divine, but an intimate and essential expression of a woman's innate connection to the sacred. The menstruation of the goddess Kamakhya is a profound symbol of the eternal flow of life, reminding devotees of the deep, transformative powers that women hold within their bodies.

The Role of Devotees and the Cultural Significance

During the Ambubachi Mela, thousands of devotees, both men and women, from all over India and beyond, gather at the Kamakhya Temple to witness the divine celebration of menstruation. For many devotees, this festival is not just about witnessing a sacred ritual, but about celebrating the divine feminine and its profound spiritual significance.

The celebration of menstruation at Kamakhya Temple serves as a powerful reminder that menstruation is not something to be hidden or shamed. Rather, it is to be celebrated as a symbol of fertility, creativity, and the deep, transformative forces that exist within all women. During the Ambubachi Mela, many women, especially those who have not experienced menstruation, perform prayers, offer flowers, and celebrate their connection to the goddess's energy.

The temple's recognition of menstruation as a sacred event empowers women to embrace their natural cycles with pride and reverence. By honoring the goddess Kamakhya's menstruation, the temple affirms the strength, fertility, and creativity inherent in every woman.

The Ambubachi Mela is not only a spiritual occasion but also a social and cultural one. Women gather together in a communal celebration, encouraging one another to recognize their inner power and to break the silence and taboo around menstruation. The festival has become a space for open discussion about the female body, menstruation, and the need to remove the stigma associated with these natural processes.

Spiritual and Scientific Significance

The spiritual importance of menstruation in Kamakhya Temple has been revered for centuries, but in contemporary times, there is also increasing recognition of the science behind the temple's practices. The sacred menstruation of Kamakhya is deeply intertwined with the physiological process of menstruation, which holds numerous health benefits for women.

One of the critical aspects of menstruation is the hormonal balance and detoxification that it brings to the female body. During menstruation, the body expels toxins and regulates hormonal levels. This process can be seen as the natural purification of the body, and in many ancient traditions, including Hinduism, menstruation is believed to symbolize the cleansing of the mind, body, and soul.

The emphasis on rest during menstruation, which is a key aspect of the Ambubachi Mela and the Kamakhya tradition, also has scientific backing. Rest allows the body to recover and reset, ensuring that the menstrual cycle operates optimally. Moreover, the psychological effects of menstruation, such as emotional fluctuations and sensitivity, are respected and honored during this sacred time, fostering mental clarity and emotional well-being.

A Global Symbol of Feminine Power

The celebration of menstruation at Kamakhya Devi Temple transcends geographical and cultural boundaries, sending a powerful message about the reverence of the female body and its inherent strength. It challenges the global narrative that often associates menstruation with impurity, shame, and silence. In contrast, the Kamakhya Temple's teachings highlight menstruation as a natural and essential process, worthy of celebration and respect.

For women, particularly in societies where menstruation is still considered a taboo, the Kamakhya Temple's celebration offers a rare and empowering model. It encourages women to connect with their own natural rhythms, embrace their bodies' divine power, and reclaim menstruation as a sacred and life-affirming force.

Conclusion: Embracing the Sacred Cycle of Life

In conclusion, the celebration of menstruation at Kamakhya Devi Temple is a powerful and transformative tradition that stands as a beacon of reverence for the divine feminine and the natural processes that govern life. The temple's recognition of menstruation as a sacred and life-affirming force challenges societal taboos, promotes the empowerment of women, and emphasizes the importance of embracing the cycle of life in all its forms.

The Kamakhya Temple serves as a reminder that menstruation is not a curse, nor a sign of impurity, but rather a natural and sacred part of life. It is a reflection of the infinite power of the goddess Kamakhya, whose energy sustains the universe and whose cycle of creation and destruction mirrors the cycles of life, death, and rebirth. By celebrating menstruation at the Kamakhya Temple, we are invited to honor and cherish the feminine power within us all.

Chapter 20:
The Meaning and Importance of the 16 Sanskaras

In Hindu tradition, life is seen as a sacred journey, from birth to death, filled with various stages of transformation, learning, and spiritual evolution. To navigate this journey, the ancient texts prescribe 16 important rituals known as *Sanskaras*—life-altering ceremonies that guide individuals through the various phases of existence, from conception to death. Each Sanskara has a profound meaning, spiritual significance, and practical purpose in ensuring a harmonious, balanced, and purposeful life.

In this chapter, we will explore the 16 *Sanskaras*, understanding their deeper spiritual significance, cultural importance, and the impact they have on an individual's life. These rites of passage are intended to purify, sanctify, and empower the individual at different points in their life, establishing them as responsible members of society while fostering a close connection with the divine.

The 16 Sanskaras: A Lifelong Journey

The 16 *Sanskaras* are spread across the entire life of an individual, covering every significant stage of growth, transformation, and maturation. They are detailed in ancient texts like the *Manu Smriti* and *Rigveda*, where they are described as rituals designed to shape the character, mind, and spirit of an individual. These rites are performed at specific points in one's life, from birth to death, guiding the individual toward a path of virtue, responsibility, and spiritual progress.

Each *Sanskara* is rooted in the belief that the soul is on a continuous journey of purification and enlightenment. These ceremonies create an opportunity for self-reflection, development, and divine connection, ensuring that every stage of life is infused with wisdom, positivity, and spiritual growth.

Let's delve into the meaning and importance of these 16 *Sanskaras*:

1. Garbhadhana (Conception Ceremony)

The first *Sanskara*, *Garbhadhana*, marks the beginning of the human journey—the moment of conception. This ritual is performed by the parents with a prayer for the birth of a healthy and virtuous child. The importance of this *Sanskara* lies in the belief that the consciousness of the child begins even before birth, and through proper invocation, the child is granted auspiciousness, wisdom, and good health. It is seen as a prayer for the soul's entry into the physical world.

2. Punsavana (Fetal Protection Ritual)

The *Punsavana* ceremony is performed during the early stages of pregnancy to ensure the health and well-being of the fetus. This rite is believed to protect the fetus from harm, ensuring its safe growth in the womb. It also invokes blessings for the unborn child's intellect and spiritual development.

3. Simantonnayana (Hair Parting Ceremony)

When a woman is in her seventh month of pregnancy, the *Simantonnayana* ritual is performed. The ceremony involves the parting of the hair of the mother, symbolizing her readiness for the birthing process. It is believed to ensure a smooth and safe delivery, while also invoking divine protection for both the mother and child.

4. Jatakarma (Birth Ritual)

The *Jatakarma* is performed immediately after the birth of the child. It involves various rites, including the child's first cry, the offering of honey, ghee, and other auspicious substances to the newborn's lips, and the chanting of Vedic mantras. This *Sanskara* marks the transition of the child into the physical world, where they are welcomed into the family and society with blessings for a long and prosperous life.

5. Namakarana (Naming Ceremony)

The *Namakarana* ceremony is performed on the 11th day or after a few weeks from birth. It involves giving the child a name, typically chosen based on astrology, cultural significance, and family traditions. The name carries a deep spiritual meaning and is believed to shape the child's destiny. It also signifies the child's individuality and place within the family and society.

6. Nishkramana (First Outing Ceremony)

This ritual is celebrated when the child is around three months old and is taken out of the house for the first time. It is a way of introducing the child to the outside world, inviting the blessings of nature and the elements. The ceremony is symbolic of the child's growing connection to the world beyond the home.

7. Annaprashana (First Feeding Ceremony)

When a child is about six months old, they are given their first solid food, usually rice. The *Annaprashana* ritual celebrates this milestone, which marks the child's transition from milk to solid food, signifying their development and growth. It is also a time for family members to offer prayers for the child's future health and prosperity.

8. Chudakarana (Hair Cutting Ceremony)

The *Chudakarana* is performed around the age of 3 years, when the child's first hair is shaved or cut. This ritual symbolizes the removal of impurities and marks the beginning of the child's journey towards spiritual growth. It is an important rite of passage in Hindu tradition, marking the first step in the child's maturity.

9. Karnavedha (Ear Piercing Ceremony)

The *Karnavedha* ceremony involves the piercing of the child's ears, typically done for both boys and girls at a young age. This ritual is believed to enhance the child's senses, particularly hearing, and is seen as a rite of passage into adulthood. It also has cultural significance, often being performed with specific prayers and blessings for the child's well-being.

10. Vidyarambha (Initiation into Education)

At the age of 5 or 7, children are initiated into education through the *Vidyarambha* ceremony. This ceremony involves the child writing their first letters or verses of a sacred text, symbolizing their entry into the world of learning. It is a ritual to encourage intellectual development and the pursuit of knowledge.

11. Upanayana (Sacred Thread Ceremony)

The *Upanayana* ceremony is one of the most significant *Sanskaras* for boys, typically performed around the age of 7 or 8. During this ritual, the child is initiated into formal education and spiritual life by receiving the sacred thread (*yajnopavita*). It marks the beginning of the child's education in sacred knowledge and religious practices, and their initiation into the responsibilities of adulthood.

12. Vedarambha (Commencement of Vedic Studies)

After the *Upanayana*, the child begins their formal study of the Vedas, typically under the guidance of a teacher or guru. The *Vedarambha* ceremony marks the commencement of this sacred learning process, signifying the child's formal entry into the world of spiritual knowledge and wisdom.

13. Keshanta (Hair Growth Ceremony)

This ceremony is performed when a child's hair reaches a certain length, often around the age of 16 for girls and 14 for boys. The *Keshanta* ritual marks the transition from childhood to adolescence, acknowledging the child's growth and maturity.

14. Vivaha (Marriage Ceremony)

The *Vivaha* ceremony is one of the most important *Sanskaras*, as it marks the union of two souls in marriage. This sacred ritual binds two individuals together, not only in body but also in spirit.

The ceremony involves the exchange of vows and blessings, with the couple committing to live together in harmony, and supporting each other in their spiritual and material pursuits.

15. Antyeshti (Funeral Rites)

The final *Sanskara*, *Antyeshti*, is performed after an individual's death. It involves the last rites and rituals to honor the deceased and ensure their soul's peaceful journey to the afterlife. These rites are crucial for the spiritual well-being of both the deceased and their family, helping to release the soul from earthly bonds and guiding it towards liberation.

16. Shraddha (Rituals for Ancestors)

The *Shraddha* ceremony is performed by descendants in honor of their ancestors, ensuring that the deceased's souls receive peace and blessings. This ritual is often performed annually on the death anniversary of loved ones, ensuring the continued connection between the living and the dead, while invoking blessings for the family's prosperity.

Conclusion: The Spiritual Path of the 16 Sanskaras

The 16 *Sanskaras* are not just rituals; they are sacred rites that mold an individual's character, purify the mind and body, and cultivate a connection with the divine. They help individuals move through life's stages with grace, spirituality, and a sense of purpose. By embracing these *Sanskaras*, one gains strength, wisdom, and an understanding of their place in the universe.

Each *Sanskara* offers an opportunity for self-realization, while also deepening one's bond with family, society, and the divine. They are a roadmap for life, guiding individuals toward ethical living, spiritual growth, and eventual liberation (*moksha*). The 16 *Sanskaras* serve as a reminder that every moment of life is sacred, and that through mindful practice, we can elevate our existence and live in harmony with the world around us.

Chapter 21:
The Science Behind Trikal Sadhana

Trikal Sadhana, the practice of mastering the three dimensions of time—past, present, and future—is a profound spiritual discipline in Hinduism that allows one to transcend the linear constraints of time. This practice involves deep meditation and inner realization, aiming to awaken a higher consciousness where the individual becomes aligned with the cosmic flow of the universe. While it is primarily a spiritual pursuit, there is a fascinating scientific aspect to this ancient technique, as it explores the interconnectedness of time, consciousness, and reality.

In this chapter, we will explore the science behind Trikal Sadhana, its relevance in modern times, and how this age-old practice can be understood through the lens of neuroscience, quantum physics, and the principles of energy.

What is Trikal Sadhana?

Trikal Sadhana refers to the meditative practice that involves understanding and manipulating the three aspects of time: past, present, and future. It is believed that through intense concentration, a practitioner can access past experiences, transcend the present moment, and glimpse into future possibilities. This practice is deeply rooted in the yogic philosophy, where time is not seen as a linear progression, but as a cyclical and multidimensional phenomenon.

In traditional texts, Trikal Sadhana is often associated with the ability to see past lives, predict future events, and understand the subtle rhythms of nature that govern human existence. It is a form of spiritual ascension, where the practitioner attains a level of consciousness that allows them to understand the greater purpose of their existence, the interconnectedness of all beings, and the nature of the universe.

The Science of Time

To understand the science behind Trikal Sadhana, we must first explore the concept of time from a scientific perspective. In modern physics, time is understood as the fourth dimension, which is intricately tied to space in the fabric of spacetime. According to Albert Einstein's theory of relativity, time is not an absolute, constant entity, but is relative to the observer's speed and position. Time can stretch and contract, depending on the observer's frame of reference. This suggests that time is not as linear and fixed as it appears to be in our day-to-day experience.

Additionally, the concept of time is deeply entwined with consciousness. Neuroscientists have found that our perception of time is not a fixed reality but is highly subjective. The brain interprets time based on external stimuli, memories, and expectations. When an individual enters deep states of meditation or altered states of consciousness, their perception of time can expand or contract. This is the foundation upon which Trikal Sadhana works—by altering the state of consciousness, one can tap into different aspects of time.

Quantum Physics and the Nature of Time

One of the most fascinating aspects of Trikal Sadhana is its potential relationship to quantum physics. In the quantum realm, particles do not follow a predictable path, and events do not unfold in a linear, deterministic way. The concept of superposition suggests that particles can exist in multiple states simultaneously, and the observer's consciousness plays a key role in determining the outcome. This aligns closely with the idea of time being non-linear and multidimensional.

Through Trikal Sadhana, practitioners may access a state of consciousness where they are no longer bound by the constraints of linear time. By becoming aware of the interconnectedness of past, present, and future, they are able to transcend the limitations of the material world and glimpse into the deeper layers of reality. This mirrors the findings in quantum physics, where the observer's consciousness influences the reality that is perceived, and where time is not fixed but fluid and changeable.

The Role of the Mind and Meditation in Trikal Sadhana

The mind plays a central role in Trikal Sadhana, as it is the vehicle through which the practitioner can navigate the dimensions of time. Meditation techniques, such as mindfulness and concentration, allow the mind to focus on the present moment, while simultaneously accessing past memories or envisioning future possibilities. This heightened state of awareness enables the practitioner to transcend the ordinary flow of time and experience it as a dynamic, ever-shifting process.

Neuroscientific research has shown that meditation can alter the brain's activity, shifting it from the default mode network (which governs day-to-day thoughts and activities) to more expansive, integrative neural networks that are associated with higher states of consciousness. In these altered states, the mind can access different aspects of time, thus aligning with the principles of Trikal Sadhana. Studies have found that regular meditation enhances the ability to recall past memories and increases intuition about future events—both of which are key components of Trikal Sadhana.

The Energy Field and Time Perception

In Hindu philosophy, it is believed that everything in the universe is composed of energy, and this energy is interconnected across all planes of existence. Each individual is part of a larger cosmic energy field, and the flow of this energy is what determines the unfolding of time. Through the practice of Trikal Sadhana, one can learn to tune into this cosmic energy field and, by doing so, gain insights into the flow of time and the events of their life.

From a scientific standpoint, this idea of energy is similar to the concept of the human biofield—the electromagnetic field produced by the body. Research has shown that the biofield plays a crucial role in maintaining health, consciousness, and perception. When a person is in deep meditation or an altered state, their biofield becomes more attuned to the surrounding energies, enabling them to perceive time in a way that is not limited by the linear structure of the physical world.

Trikal Sadhana and the Art of Decision Making

One of the most profound aspects of Trikal Sadhana is its potential to guide decision-making. When an individual practices this meditation, they can gain clarity about past mistakes, present actions, and future consequences. This ability to view time holistically can help individuals make better decisions, as they understand the broader context and the karmic consequences of their actions. It also helps them to move beyond the limitations of fear and anxiety, as they are able to recognize the interconnectedness of all things and trust in the cosmic flow.

Practical Applications of Trikal Sadhana in Modern Life

While Trikal Sadhana may seem esoteric, its principles have practical applications in daily life. By learning to still the mind and focus on the present moment, individuals can gain a deeper understanding of their past experiences, make wiser decisions in the present, and shape a more harmonious future. The ability to reflect on past experiences without attachment or regret, and to envision a future filled with possibilities, is a powerful tool for personal growth and transformation.

Moreover, by accessing the deeper layers of consciousness, individuals can gain a greater sense of purpose and direction in their life, free from the constraints of societal pressures and expectations. This can lead to a more fulfilling and spiritually rich life.

Conclusion: A Path to Higher Consciousness

Trikal Sadhana is more than just a meditation practice—it is a journey toward mastering time and transcending the limitations of the physical world. Through this ancient discipline, practitioners can access higher states of consciousness, gain clarity and insight, and align themselves with the cosmic flow of the universe. The science behind Trikal Sadhana is rooted in principles of quantum physics, neuroscience, and energy, all of which converge to reveal the profound interconnectedness of time, consciousness, and the universe.

By understanding and practicing Trikal Sadhana, individuals can transform their perception of time, transcend the ordinary limitations of their existence, and step into a higher realm of awareness and spiritual growth. This timeless practice offers a path to self-realization, inner peace, and an expanded understanding of the universe and the self.

Chapter 22:
The Science Behind Chanting AUM

AUM (also spelled OM) is one of the most sacred and powerful sounds in Hinduism, considered the primordial sound of the universe. It is not just a mantra but a universal symbol of the infinite, the eternal, and the supreme reality—Brahman. AUM is seen as the source from which everything emanates and the vibration that pervades all of existence. Chanting AUM is a practice that goes beyond spiritual significance, with a rich connection to the physical, emotional, and mental aspects of our being. In this chapter, we explore the profound science behind chanting AUM and how it influences the body, mind, and consciousness.

The Sacred Sound of AUM

AUM is a composite of three syllables—A, U, and M—each representing different aspects of the universe and consciousness.

1. **A (अ)** – This sound represents the waking state, symbolizing creation, beginning, and the physical world. It is said to be the first sound of creation, corresponding to the physical reality.

2. **U (उ)** – This sound represents the dreaming state, symbolizing the manifestation of desires, intuition, and subtle experiences. It connects us to the inner world, the subconscious, and the world of ideas.

3. **M (म)** – This sound represents the deep sleep state, symbolizing the state of pure consciousness, the unmanifested, and the ultimate reality. It is considered the sound of dissolution, where all form merges back into the infinite.

Together, these three syllables encompass the three states of human consciousness (waking, dreaming, and deep sleep), as well as the past, present, and future, symbolizing the totality of existence.

The silence that follows the chanting of AUM is equally significant. It represents the fourth state, known as **Turiya**, the state of transcendental consciousness. It is a state of pure bliss and realization where the individual becomes one with the universe. This silence is not a mere absence of sound but is seen as the subtle vibration that connects one with the infinite.

The Vibrational Impact of AUM on the Body

The sound of AUM is not just a spiritual tool, but it also has a significant impact on the physical body. Sound, in general, is a form of energy that affects the vibrations of the matter. AUM, being the sound of the universe itself, resonates with every cell in our body.

1. **Vibrations and Frequency**: The sound of AUM is believed to vibrate at a frequency that aligns with the natural frequencies of the universe. These vibrations travel through the body, aligning and harmonizing the energies within. Studies in the field of sound therapy and vibrational medicine show that sound frequencies have the power to heal, balance, and energize the body. By chanting AUM, the body is exposed to a frequency that promotes physical well-being.

2. **Resonance with the Nervous System**: The act of chanting AUM affects the nervous system, helping to induce a state of relaxation. The deep, steady sound of AUM slows down the breath and reduces the heart rate, leading to a reduction in stress and anxiety. It has been observed that chanting this sound can activate the parasympathetic nervous system (the rest-and-digest response), leading to a sense of calm and tranquility.

3. **Breath and Pranayama**: The practice of chanting AUM is closely related to breath control (pranayama). As the sound is prolonged, the breath becomes slow, deep, and rhythmic. This controlled breathing oxygenates the body, helps in detoxification, and promotes a sense of balance. Proper breath control has been scientifically linked to improved mental clarity, emotional stability, and physical health.

The Scientific Explanation of the Sound Frequency

Every sound has a specific frequency, and it is believed that the frequency of AUM (approximately 432 Hz) aligns with the natural frequency of the universe. This frequency is said to have a harmonizing effect on the body and the environment. In fact, many spiritual traditions and healing modalities use this frequency to bring about healing and alignment within the body.

Research in the field of sound healing shows that certain frequencies, such as 432 Hz, have a positive impact on the human body. These frequencies are believed to resonate with the body's cells and energy fields, helping to restore balance and harmony. AUM's frequency aligns with the vibrations of nature, which can have a profound impact on the practitioner's state of mind, body, and spirit.

AUM and the Brain

Chanting AUM has a direct impact on the brain. Neuroscientific studies on the effects of sound on the brain have shown that chanting or listening to certain sounds can lead to changes in brainwave activity. When AUM is chanted, it has been shown to stimulate the alpha brainwaves—those associated with relaxation, calm, and meditation. This is the same brainwave pattern that occurs when we are deeply relaxed or in a meditative state.

1. **Alpha Brainwaves**: Alpha waves are associated with a relaxed but focused state of mind. These waves help reduce stress, anxiety, and mental fatigue. They also encourage

creativity and mental clarity. Chanting AUM regularly can help bring the brain into an alpha state, promoting overall well-being and emotional stability.

2. **Theta Brainwaves**: In deeper states of meditation, chanting AUM can also stimulate theta brainwaves, which are linked to deep meditation, intuition, and access to the subconscious mind. Theta waves are often associated with higher states of consciousness, healing, and spiritual experiences.

3. **Endorphin Release**: Studies have found that chanting AUM can lead to the release of endorphins, the body's natural "feel-good" hormones. This contributes to a sense of peace and happiness, helping to reduce stress and uplift the spirit.

Spiritual and Mental Benefits of Chanting AUM

On a spiritual level, chanting AUM is said to help the practitioner connect with their higher self, the divine, and the universal consciousness. It is believed to be a sound that transcends the ego and connects the individual with the eternal. In the practice of Trataka (concentration) and meditation, AUM is often used to focus the mind and bring it into a state of pure awareness.

1. **Mindfulness and Presence**: Chanting AUM allows the practitioner to become more present in the moment. By focusing on the sound and vibration of AUM, one can transcend distractions and mental chatter. This deep concentration fosters mindfulness, enabling the individual to be fully immersed in the experience of the present moment.

2. **Emotional Balance**: Chanting AUM has been shown to help balance emotions by calming the nervous system and clearing negative energy. It is a powerful tool for releasing emotional blockages, reducing anger, and alleviating depression and anxiety. The rhythmic and harmonious nature of AUM brings emotional healing and inner peace.

3. **Spiritual Connection**: For practitioners of spiritual traditions, chanting AUM serves as a bridge between the

individual self and the higher self, the material world, and the spiritual realm. It is said to awaken dormant spiritual energies within the body, connecting the practitioner to divine consciousness. This deep connection is essential for self-realization and spiritual growth.

Conclusion: The Unifying Power of AUM

AUM is much more than just a mantra or sound; it is the essence of creation itself. The science behind chanting AUM lies in its ability to affect the body, mind, and consciousness. From its vibrational frequency, which aligns with the natural energies of the universe, to its impact on brainwave activity, the act of chanting AUM promotes healing, relaxation, and spiritual awakening. It brings the practitioner into harmony with the natural world and the cosmic order, allowing for a deeper connection with the self and the divine.

By incorporating the practice of chanting AUM into daily life, one can experience a profound shift in consciousness, physical well-being, and emotional balance. AUM, as the sound of the universe, is a powerful tool for achieving peace, clarity, and spiritual growth, connecting the individual with the infinite and the eternal.

Chapter 23:
The Importance of Kapoor Aarti at the End of Puja

The Kapoor Aarti, often performed at the conclusion of a religious puja (ritual), is a significant practice in Hindu worship. Kapoor, or camphor, is widely used during the aarti ceremony, especially at the end, to offer the final devotion to the deity. The lighted camphor symbolizes the illumination of the soul and the burning away of negativity. This chapter explores the profound significance of Kapoor Aarti, both from a spiritual and scientific perspective, and why it is considered an essential part of the puja ritual.

Understanding Kapoor Aarti

Kapoor Aarti is a ritual where camphor is lit in front of the deity at the end of the puja, accompanied by the chanting of prayers and the ringing of bells. The aarti is typically performed with great devotion, as the bright flame of camphor is offered as an expression of purity and surrender to the divine. The camphor flame is a symbol of the soul's journey toward enlightenment, burning away the darkness of ignorance and illusion.

Spiritual Significance of Kapoor Aarti

1. **Symbolizing the Light of Knowledge**: In Hinduism, light is often associated with knowledge, wisdom, and the presence of the divine. The flame of camphor is seen as the representation of Lord Shiva's pure and eternal light, which dispels ignorance and brings clarity. The light from the camphor is believed to purify the atmosphere and the minds of the worshippers, leading them closer to spiritual liberation.

2. **Surrendering to the Divine**: Offering camphor in the form of a flame symbolizes the devotee's surrender to God. Just as

the flame is fleeting and dissipates into the air, it is a reminder of the temporary nature of the physical body and the material world. The camphor, when lit, burns completely, signifying the devotee's desire to offer their ego and material desires to the divine, thus attaining self-realization and spiritual freedom.

3. **Purification of the Environment**: The act of burning camphor is also seen as a means of purifying the space where the puja is conducted. Camphor is known for its antiseptic properties and is believed to cleanse the environment of negative energies and vibrations. As the flame burns, the area is thought to be filled with divine energy, creating a serene and sacred space for spiritual connection.

4. **Offering Devotion with a Pure Heart**: Kapoor Aarti represents the culmination of the puja, where the devotee offers their most pure and sincere devotion to the deity. The camphor, when burned, emits a soft, radiant glow, symbolizing the purity of the heart and the soul's longing for union with the divine. The light from the camphor represents the spiritual illumination that comes from devotion and prayer.

The Role of Camphor in Kapoor Aarti

Camphor, also known as **"karpur"**, is a natural substance derived from the wood of the camphor tree. It has a strong, pleasant fragrance and is used extensively in religious rituals. The significance of camphor in the Aarti can be explored from both a practical and spiritual perspective:

1. **Fragrance and Spiritual Elevation**: The fragrant smoke produced by burning camphor is believed to purify the air and elevate the spiritual energy in the environment. The fragrance is uplifting, and its strong, fresh aroma is thought to clear the mind and help devotees enter a higher state of consciousness. It is said that the scent of camphor during the Aarti symbolizes the sweet presence of the divine.

2. **Burning Away of Negative Energy**: Scientifically, camphor has properties that help to purify the air. It is a natural antiseptic and is believed to reduce air pollution and create a more positive and soothing environment. Spiritually, it is seen as having the power to burn away negative energies, thoughts, and emotions, creating a space for positive energy to flow.

3. **Symbol of Transcendence**: The camphor flame, with its delicate and intense burning, is a symbol of the soul's journey toward transcendence. Just as the flame burns brightly and disappears, it signifies the detachment from the material world and the desire to merge with the eternal truth. The burning away of the camphor represents the dissolution of the ego, which is necessary for spiritual progress.

4. **A Meditation Tool**: The camphor flame is often used as a focus for meditation. As devotees chant prayers and offer the Aarti, their minds focus on the flame, which helps quiet the mind and brings about a state of inner peace. The radiant flame serves as a reminder of the divine presence and the ultimate goal of merging with the infinite light.

The Ritual of Kapoor Aarti

Kapoor Aarti is typically performed as the final act of a puja. It is a moment of divine connection, where the worshippers offer their heartfelt devotion and prayers. The ritual follows a specific process:

1. **Preparation of Camphor**: Camphor is usually placed in a small metal plate or holder, and a wick or cotton thread is used to light it. The camphor can be purchased in various forms, but it is often in solid cubes or liquid form that is poured onto the wick.

2. **Lighting the Camphor**: The priest or devotee lights the camphor using a flame. As the camphor catches fire, it produces a bright, radiant light that symbolizes the divine

presence. The camphor flame is held in front of the deity, and the devotee offers their prayers and gratitude.

3. **Chanting and Offering Prayers**: While the camphor burns, the priest or devotees may chant specific mantras or prayers, calling upon the deity to accept their devotion. The chanting is accompanied by the ringing of bells, which is a traditional way of invoking divine blessings.

4. **Circling the Flame**: The camphor flame is often moved in circular motions in front of the deity. This process is known as "aarti" and is meant to invoke the divine presence and energize the atmosphere. The flame is usually offered in a clockwise direction, symbolizing the flow of energy from the individual to the divine.

5. **Conclusion of the Ritual**: After the camphor has burned out completely, the Aarti concludes with a final prayer or offering. The devotees may bow down, take the blessings of the deity, and feel a sense of spiritual fulfillment.

The Benefits of Kapoor Aarti

1. **Emotional Healing**: The practice of performing Kapoor Aarti is believed to bring emotional healing. As the camphor burns, it is thought to release stress, anxiety, and emotional blockages. The act of offering the Aarti and focusing on the flame helps to create a sense of peace and tranquility.

2. **Spiritual Growth**: By performing Kapoor Aarti with devotion, the individual is thought to invite spiritual progress. The flame of camphor serves as a guide, illuminating the path to self-realization and spiritual enlightenment.

3. **Manifestation of Divine Energy**: The Aarti ceremony is an opportunity to invoke divine energy. The ritual is seen as an act of deep devotion, where the devotee surrenders to the divine and receives blessings in the form of peace, prosperity, and wisdom.

Conclusion: The Sacred Power of Kapoor Aarti

Kapoor Aarti is not just an aesthetic ritual; it is a spiritual practice that helps purify the body, mind, and environment. The burning of camphor symbolizes the light of divine consciousness, the purification of the soul, and the detachment from material desires. Through this simple yet profound ritual, devotees offer their prayers, gratitude, and devotion, while also receiving the blessings of the divine. Kapoor Aarti serves as a reminder of the transience of life, the illumination of knowledge, and the ultimate goal of spiritual liberation.

The science behind Kapoor Aarti lies in its ability to cleanse and elevate the energy in the environment, while its spiritual significance helps to foster devotion, peace, and connection with the divine. It is a powerful way to end a puja, leaving the worshippers with a sense of calm, fulfillment, and divine grace.

Chapter 24:
Why Do We Sprinkle Water Around Food Before Eating?

In many Indian households, a common ritual before eating is to sprinkle water around the food or on the plate. While this practice may seem like a simple gesture, it holds deep significance from both spiritual and scientific perspectives. In this chapter, we explore the reasons behind this custom, shedding light on its cultural, religious, and scientific aspects.

Spiritual and Religious Significance

1. **Purification of Food**: One of the primary reasons behind sprinkling water around food is the belief in purifying the food before consumption. In Hinduism, food is considered sacred, and it is believed to carry energy that can affect the body and mind. Sprinkling water around food is thought to purify it from any negative energy, and it ensures that the food is fit for consumption. This ritual is often accompanied by prayers or gratitude toward the deity, acknowledging the divinity that has made the food possible.

2. **Acknowledgment of the Divine**: In many traditions, food is seen as a divine offering. It is believed that by performing certain rituals, such as sprinkling water, one can create a sacred environment for the food. This is a way of recognizing that food sustains life and should be treated with reverence. The sprinkling of water is a simple yet powerful act of paying respect to the nourishment provided by nature, and by invoking the divine in the process, it is thought to enhance the food's spiritual potency.

3. **Symbol of Humility**: The practice of sprinkling water around food can also be seen as a symbol of humility and gratitude. It is a reminder that we are not superior to the food

we consume, but instead, we must show respect to it as a gift from the universe. The water, which represents purity, is used to cleanse and sanctify the food, ensuring that the act of eating is done with respect and mindfulness.

4. **Connection to Sacred Rituals**: In various religious rituals, water is considered a purifying element. Just as water is used in sacred rites to cleanse spaces or people, its use in food rituals extends the same concept of purification. Before a meal, water is sprinkled to create an auspicious setting for consuming the food, with the belief that it enhances the blessings and spiritual benefits of the meal.

Scientific and Health Reasons

1. **Removal of Impurities**: From a scientific point of view, sprinkling water around food can help to remove any impurities that might be present. Water, when sprayed lightly, can wash away dust, microbes, and other contaminants that might have settled on the food or utensils. This practice can be especially important in areas where food is prepared outdoors or in environments where hygiene may be a concern. In this sense, sprinkling water can be viewed as an early form of hygiene, helping to clean the food before consumption.

2. **Enhancing Food's Freshness**: Water is known to preserve the freshness of food. When sprinkled on fruits, vegetables, or dry foods, it can help in retaining moisture, preventing them from drying out, and maintaining their nutritional quality. In some cases, sprinkling water around food can also bring out the aroma, enhancing the sensory experience of the meal.

3. **Activating the Food's Energy**: According to ancient Indian traditions and Ayurveda, food carries energy that can impact the body. The food is believed to be infused with various energies, such as sattvic (pure), rajasic (active), or tamasic (dull). Sprinkling water around the food is thought to

activate the sattvic energy, making the food more beneficial for health and well-being. The action of sprinkling water is said to activate and balance the energies in the food, helping to align them with the body's needs.

4. **Creating a Positive Environment for Eating**: Another practical explanation for sprinkling water around food is that it helps create a serene and peaceful environment for the meal. In many cultures, eating is seen not just as a physical activity but as a spiritual one. The presence of water around the food can enhance the ambiance, encouraging mindfulness during the meal. The gentle act of sprinkling water before eating can help the person to focus on the food and foster a sense of calm, which aids in digestion and overall health.

5. **Hydration**: Water is essential for hydration, and while the food we consume provides much of the nourishment, water aids in the body's absorption and digestion process. By sprinkling water around the food, one may be subconsciously reminding themselves to stay hydrated, as it is often the case that food is accompanied by a glass of water during meals.

Cultural and Regional Variations

The custom of sprinkling water around food is observed in various forms across different regions and cultures. While it holds similar meanings of purification, respect, and gratitude, the specific rituals and practices can vary:

- **In South India**, it is common to sprinkle water on the plate before serving food as a gesture of cleaning and purification.
- **In the North**, the custom of sprinkling water is often observed in temples and during formal meals, especially when offering food to the deity.
- **In some spiritual practices**, water is used to cleanse the utensils or the space where the meal will be served, ensuring

that the food is being consumed in an auspicious and pure environment.

Connection to the Five Elements

The use of water in the ritual of sprinkling around food also connects to the belief in the five elements (earth, water, fire, air, and ether) that are integral to Hindu philosophy. Water represents purification and cleansing, and its presence enhances the harmony of the other elements in the food. By sprinkling water around food, one is thought to be balancing and aligning the food with the energies of the earth, ensuring that the nourishment is complete and holistic.

Conclusion: The Sacredness of the Act

The simple act of sprinkling water around food before eating goes beyond the surface and touches upon the spiritual, cultural, and scientific realms. It serves as a reminder of our interconnectedness with nature, our responsibility to show respect for the sustenance we receive, and the importance of maintaining purity in both body and mind. By understanding the significance of this practice, we can approach our meals with a greater sense of mindfulness, gratitude, and reverence. The ritual is not just about food; it is about honoring life itself, acknowledging the source of nourishment, and creating a positive, sacred atmosphere that enriches the meal and our overall well-being.

Chapter 25:
Meaning and Significance of the Gayatri Mantra

The Gayatri Mantra, one of the most revered and powerful mantras in Hinduism, holds profound significance both spiritually and scientifically. It is a sacred invocation that is chanted by millions across the world, invoking divine energy and seeking the blessings of the Supreme Creator. This chapter delves into the meaning, origin, and scientific relevance of the Gayatri Mantra, shedding light on its importance in daily spiritual practices.

The Meaning of the Gayatri Mantra

The Gayatri Mantra is composed of 24 syllables and is attributed to the sage Vishwamitra, who is said to have received the mantra during his deep meditation. It is found in the Rigveda (3.62.10), one of the oldest and most sacred texts of Hinduism. The mantra is as follows:

"Om Bhur Bhuvah Swaha,

Tat Savitur Varenyam,

Bhargo Devasya Dhimahi,

Dhiyo Yo Nah Prachodayat."

Breaking down the meaning of this powerful mantra:

- **"Om"**: The universal sound or vibration that symbolizes the ultimate reality, consciousness, or the Supreme Being.
- **"Bhur"**: The physical realm or the Earth. It represents the material world, our existence on the Earth plane.
- **"Bhuvah"**: The mental realm or the atmosphere. It refers to the space between the physical and spiritual realms, where thoughts, emotions, and energies are transmitted.

- **"Swaha"**: The celestial realm or the heaven. It signifies the higher spiritual planes and the divinity that resides beyond the material world.
- **"Tat"**: That supreme, eternal reality. It refers to the divine consciousness or the ultimate truth that transcends all physical and mental realms.
- **"Savitur"**: The divine light or the sun, symbolizing the source of all energy, wisdom, and enlightenment.
- **"Varenyam"**: Worthy of praise and reverence. It is an invocation to the divine light to illuminate our hearts and minds.
- **"Bhargo"**: The divine essence or the radiant, purifying energy that cleanses and elevates the individual.
- **"Devasya"**: Of the deity, referring to the divine source from which all wisdom and light emanate.
- **"Dhimahi"**: We meditate upon, we absorb the divine energy.
- **"Dhiyo"**: The intellect or understanding. It refers to the higher, enlightened consciousness.
- **"Yo Nah"**: May that divine light, energy, and wisdom shine upon us.
- **"Prachodayat"**: May it inspire, guide, and direct our thoughts and actions towards righteousness and truth.

In essence, the Gayatri Mantra is an invocation to the Supreme Creator, asking for enlightenment, wisdom, and guidance to transcend the limitations of the material world and achieve a state of higher consciousness.

The Spiritual Significance

1. **Invocation of Divine Light**: The Gayatri Mantra is primarily a prayer for the awakening of the soul, intellect, and

consciousness. By chanting this mantra, devotees seek the divine light to guide them through the darkness of ignorance and lead them to enlightenment. It is believed that by meditating on this mantra, one aligns themselves with the universal consciousness, bringing peace, harmony, and clarity into their lives.

2. **Purification of Mind and Body**: The mantra is a purifying force that works on the mind, body, and soul. It helps in cleansing the impurities of the mind, dispelling negative thoughts, and promoting inner peace. Through the regular chanting of the Gayatri Mantra, one is believed to be able to remove mental clutter and attain a tranquil state of mind.

3. **Connection to the Supreme**: The Gayatri Mantra helps establish a direct connection with the Supreme Being. It is a prayer that unites the individual with the cosmic energy, transcending the limitations of time and space. The chanting of this mantra is believed to elevate the practitioner spiritually and bring them closer to the divine source of creation.

4. **Enhancing Wisdom and Intellect**: The mantra invokes the blessing of wisdom and intellect, helping the devotee achieve clarity in their thoughts and actions. It is said to enhance cognitive abilities and awaken the higher faculties of the brain, allowing one to make better decisions and act in alignment with their higher self.

Scientific Perspective

While the Gayatri Mantra has been revered as a spiritual practice for centuries, modern science has begun to explore the potential benefits of sound vibrations and their effects on the human mind and body. The Gayatri Mantra, with its precise combination of sounds, syllables, and rhythms, is believed to have several positive effects on the practitioner.

1. **Vibrational Energy**: Every sound has a specific frequency and vibrational energy. The Gayatri Mantra, when chanted aloud, produces sound waves that resonate with the energy centers (chakras) in the body. These vibrations have a calming and balancing effect on the mind and body, promoting physical, emotional, and mental well-being.

2. **Stress Reduction**: Chanting the Gayatri Mantra can lead to a state of deep relaxation. The rhythmic repetition of the sounds helps slow down the brainwaves, putting the mind in a meditative state. This has been shown to reduce stress, anxiety, and negative emotions, enhancing overall mental health.

3. **Positive Impact on Brain Function**: The rhythmic chanting of the Gayatri Mantra stimulates the left and right hemispheres of the brain, helping to increase concentration, improve memory, and boost cognitive abilities. Scientific studies have shown that mantra chanting can lead to improvements in brainwave patterns, particularly in the alpha and theta frequencies, which are associated with relaxation and creativity.

4. **Healing Vibrations**: Some studies suggest that the vibrations created by chanting the Gayatri Mantra have healing properties. The mantra is thought to produce vibrations that can harmonize the body's energy, promote cellular regeneration, and strengthen the immune system. The chanting of the mantra is believed to support physical health by promoting balance and stability in the body.

The Global Influence of the Gayatri Mantra

The Gayatri Mantra has transcended cultural and geographical boundaries and has been embraced by people from various parts of the world. It is considered universal, as its message of spiritual awakening and enlightenment resonates with individuals regardless of their religious or cultural background. In addition to its use in Hinduism, the Gayatri Mantra is practiced by people seeking peace, well-being, and a connection to the divine.

Many spiritual teachers and organizations around the world promote the chanting of the Gayatri Mantra for its calming effects and its ability to promote higher consciousness. In recent years, the mantra has gained popularity in meditation and yoga practices as a tool for spiritual growth and self-improvement.

Conclusion: The Timeless Power of the Gayatri Mantra

The Gayatri Mantra is more than just a chant; it is a profound expression of the longing for divine knowledge and enlightenment. Its meaning encompasses the aspiration for spiritual awakening, mental clarity, and the ultimate realization of the self's connection to the supreme consciousness. Whether viewed from a spiritual, philosophical, or scientific perspective, the Gayatri Mantra offers powerful benefits that help individuals navigate the complexities of life with wisdom, peace, and harmony. By chanting this ancient mantra, practitioners can invite divine blessings into their lives, fostering growth in both the material and spiritual realms.

Chapter 26:
Science Behind Offering Coconut in Temple

Offering coconuts in temples is a common practice in Hindu rituals, signifying devotion, humility, and the act of surrendering one's ego to the divine. It holds deep spiritual significance, symbolizing purity, selflessness, and the breaking of the ego, which is believed to be the barrier to divine connection. But beyond its religious and symbolic meaning, there is also a scientific rationale behind offering coconuts that can be understood through the lens of Ayurveda, energy exchange, and environmental science. This chapter delves into the science behind the practice of offering coconuts in temples, unraveling both its spiritual and scientific significance.

Symbolism and Spiritual Meaning of Coconut

In Hinduism, the coconut is considered a symbol of the human body and mind. The tough outer shell represents the physical body, the white inner flesh symbolizes the mind, and the water inside represents the soul. The offering of a coconut in a temple is seen as an offering of one's ego. When devotees break the coconut, they symbolically break their ego, offering themselves in surrender to the divine. This represents a transformation, where one's inner self is purified and elevated through the ritual.

- **Outer Shell (Body)**: The tough shell of the coconut symbolizes the body, which encases the soul. It is often likened to the human ego—hard and protective. When the coconut is broken, it represents the breaking of the ego, which allows the divine energy to enter and purify the soul.

- **Inner Flesh (Mind)**: The soft, tender flesh of the coconut represents the mind, which is meant to be humble and pure. By offering the coconut, the devotee purifies their thoughts and surrenders them to the divine will.

- **Water (Soul)**: The water inside the coconut symbolizes the soul, which is considered sacred. Offering the coconut to the deity is seen as offering one's soul to the divine.

Through this offering, devotees not only honor the divine but also seek to purify themselves by breaking their ego and surrendering their desires, worries, and attachments.

Scientific Significance of Offering Coconut

1. **Electromagnetic Energy and Resonance**: Coconuts are known to possess high electrical conductivity. The water inside a coconut is a good conductor of electromagnetic energy, and it is believed that the act of offering a coconut creates an exchange of energy between the devotee and the temple environment. The coconut can absorb and amplify the energies present in the sacred space, which can positively impact the person offering it.

   When the coconut is cracked open during the ritual, the energy within it is released into the environment. The breaking of the coconut thus symbolizes the release of negative energy, which is thought to cleanse the surroundings and the individual.

2. **Coconut and Ayurveda**: Ayurveda, the ancient system of medicine, places great importance on natural elements, and coconuts are considered highly auspicious in this practice. According to Ayurveda, coconuts have cooling properties and are beneficial for balancing the body's three doshas—Vata, Pitta, and Kapha.

   a. **Cooling Effect**: The coconut's water and pulp are considered cooling for the body and mind. When offered during rituals, it is believed that the coconut's inherent cooling properties help to calm the mind and restore balance within the person.

   b. **Nutrient-Rich**: The coconut's water contains minerals such as potassium, sodium, calcium, and magnesium. Offering a coconut symbolizes the nourishment of the soul and spirit, much like how food nourishes the body. It is also believed that coconut water is purifying for the body, symbolizing physical and spiritual purification during the ritual.

3. **Purification and Healing**: Coconuts, with their natural properties, are also believed to purify the air and the space. In ancient times, temples were built in areas where fresh air and natural resources like coconuts were abundant. Offering a coconut, especially in the early morning or during important religious festivals, was seen as a way to connect with nature and enhance the spiritual experience.

The coconut is also considered to possess a protective energy. The hard outer shell is thought to act as a shield, protecting the devotee from negative energies and ill-health. By offering the coconut, devotees are believed to receive divine protection and blessings.

4. **Environmental Science and Sustainability**: The coconut tree is often referred to as the "tree of life" because it is an incredibly versatile plant. From the water and flesh to the outer husk and leaves, every part of the coconut can be used for various purposes. This makes the coconut an environmentally sustainable offering in temples, as it supports a zero-waste philosophy.

The coconut water, which is used for purification rituals, also has a beneficial impact on the environment. When offered in temples, the coconut water and the coconut's remains are often used in a manner that is ecologically sustainable. Leftover parts of the coconut are used in composting or as animal feed, ensuring that nothing goes to waste.

5. **Symbolic of Generosity**: In many cultures, the coconut is seen as a symbol of generosity and abundance. The offering of a coconut to the deity is seen as a gesture of giving from the devotee's heart. Scientifically, giving is an act that activates certain neural pathways in the brain that promote happiness and well-being. By offering something as valuable

as a coconut, devotees not only seek the blessings of the divine but also foster a sense of gratitude and positive energy in their own lives.

Psychological Impact of Coconut Offering

The act of offering a coconut also has psychological benefits. For many, the ritual of offering a coconut helps to release anxiety, stress, and negative emotions. The simple act of breaking the coconut—an act of surrendering the ego—helps to bring clarity and peace to the mind. The devotee's focus shifts from worldly concerns to spiritual devotion, creating a sense of inner peace and contentment.

Additionally, this act of surrender and offering symbolizes a fresh start, much like the water inside the coconut. The ritual of offering the coconut represents new beginnings, renewal, and the elimination of negative thoughts, leaving space for positive energy and divine blessings.

Conclusion: The Holistic Significance of Offering Coconut

Offering a coconut in temples goes beyond mere tradition or religious practice—it is an act that intertwines spiritual, scientific, and psychological benefits. From a symbolic standpoint, it represents the surrender of the ego and the offering of one's self to the divine. Scientifically, the coconut's inherent properties help to purify the space, enhance positive energy, and promote balance within the individual. Psychologically, the act of offering fosters peace, gratitude, and a sense of connection to both the divine and the natural world.

Thus, offering a coconut in temples serves as a powerful reminder of our connection to nature, the divine, and ourselves. It is a ritual that not only purifies the soul but also helps us to foster spiritual growth, well-being, and harmony with the world around us.

Chapter 27:
Meaning and Importance of Swastik

The **Swastik** symbol is one of the most ancient and significant symbols in Hindu culture. It has been used for centuries, not just in India, but across different civilizations. It represents auspiciousness, prosperity, and good fortune. The Swastik symbol has a profound spiritual and scientific meaning, which goes beyond its religious significance.

Meaning of Swastik

The word "Swastik" is derived from the Sanskrit word **"Swasti"**, which means "well-being," "prosperity," or "good fortune." It is a symbol formed by four arms, which are usually bent at 90 degrees, often drawn in a clockwise direction, though it can also be seen in a counterclockwise form, especially in certain tantric practices.

The Swastik can be visualized as:

- **Four arms** representing the four cardinal directions: North, South, East, and West.

- **The central point** symbolizes the source of energy, the cosmic center from which everything originates.

- **The right-angled bends** symbolize stability and progress, the notion of growth in life, or a foundation from which one can build.

In Hinduism, the Swastik is sacred and considered to be a symbol of Lord Ganesha, who represents the removal of obstacles, and also symbolizes the Sun, which is a source of life and energy for all living beings.

Spiritual Significance of Swastik

The Swastik is a symbol of **positive energy** and **good fortune**. It is believed that it represents the cosmic order of life, in the sense that the universe, nature, and life itself have a rhythm and balance. This rhythm is represented by the four arms of the Swastik, signifying the **four stages of life**: birth, youth, maturity, and death. When aligned with the natural forces, this symbol promotes harmony and well-being.

- **Symbol of Ganesha**: In many Hindu homes, Swastik is drawn before starting any auspicious occasion or new venture to invoke the blessings of Lord Ganesha, who is known as the remover of obstacles. Swastik is often seen on doors, walls, and invitation cards as an emblem of auspiciousness.

- **A Connection to the Sun**: The Swastik also represents the movement of the Sun. It is symbolic of the **Sun's rotation** in the sky, representing the eternal flow of time, light, and life-giving energy. In this sense, the symbol is a reminder of the eternal cycles of life and cosmic rhythms.

The Scientific Significance of Swastik

Beyond its spiritual connotations, the Swastik also has **scientific significance**:

1. **Energy Flow**: The clockwise motion of the Swastik symbol is said to represent the flow of energy in the universe. The clockwise direction is associated with **positive energy** and **growth**, whereas the counterclockwise direction, often seen in tantric practices, symbolizes **inner transformation** and **spiritual awakening**.

2. **Magnetic Field Representation**: Some studies and interpretations link the Swastik with **magnetic fields**. The arms of the Swastik are seen to represent the flow of magnetic energy from the center, helping to direct positive

energy into the surroundings. This has been particularly significant in the construction of temples, homes, and altars, where the positioning of the Swastik was done in such a way that it ensured the optimal flow of cosmic energy.

3. **Alignment with Vastu Shastra**: In **Vastu Shastra** (the ancient science of architecture), the Swastik is considered an auspicious symbol. Its placement in the home is believed to bring prosperity and balance to the living space. The symmetrical arms of the Swastik help maintain balance and the flow of positive energy throughout a building.

Swastik in Daily Life and Rituals

1. **Celebrations and Festivals**: Swastik is widely used during religious ceremonies, especially during festivals like Diwali and Gudi Padwa. It is drawn on doors and walls to ensure that the coming year is filled with prosperity and positivity.

2. **Weddings and Auspicious Occasions**: During weddings, the Swastik symbol is used to mark the beginning of a new journey. It is drawn on invitation cards, wedding attire, and even the marriage altar as a sign of good luck and protection.

3. **Temples and Sacred Spaces**: In temples, the Swastik is often drawn on the threshold to ward off negative energies and invite positive vibrations. The symbol represents the divine presence of the deities and ensures spiritual safety for the devotees.

4. **Religious Offerings**: During religious rituals, Swastik is used in offerings and rituals to mark the sacredness of the occasion and to invite the blessings of deities for abundance and success.

Cultural Significance

The Swastik transcends religious boundaries. It has been used as a symbol of well-being in several cultures, including ancient Greece, China, and Europe. In fact, it was commonly used in the

Western world until the 20th century, where it was associated with positive connotations such as prosperity, peace, and the cyclical nature of life.

In modern-day India, the Swastik remains an important symbol of spirituality and a reminder of the **universal truth** that all things are interconnected and interdependent.

Conclusion

The **Swastik** is not just a symbol; it is a representation of the **balance of cosmic energy** and the **divine order** of the universe. Whether in its use for religious purposes or its role in modern scientific interpretations, the Swastik carries a profound message of positivity, stability, and divine protection. By understanding its deeper meanings, we can incorporate its significance into our daily lives to lead a path of spiritual growth, prosperity, and balance.

Chapter 28:
Meaning and Importance of Rituals After Death

Death is an inevitable part of life, and it is considered one of the most significant transitions in the human journey. While the physical body ceases to exist, the soul is believed to continue its journey, and it is essential to ensure that the soul is at peace and guided properly to its next stage. In Hindu tradition, various rituals after death are performed with the intent to honor the departed soul, ensure its peace, and help it transition smoothly to the afterlife. These rituals have deep cultural, spiritual, and scientific significance.

The Purpose of Death Rituals

The rituals performed after death are not merely symbolic; they are deeply rooted in both spiritual beliefs and psychological needs. The primary purposes of these rituals are:

1. **To Honor the Departed Soul**: It is believed that the soul continues to exist after the physical death, and these rituals help honor and acknowledge the contributions of the deceased during their lifetime. They provide an opportunity for loved ones to express gratitude, respect, and love.

2. **To Guide the Soul**: It is said that the soul of the deceased may linger or may be confused after death. The rituals help guide the soul on its journey, ensuring that it moves on peacefully and without hindrance. The rites serve as a way to help the soul reach its final destination, whether it be rebirth or moksha (liberation).

3. **To Provide Closure for the Family**: Death is an emotionally challenging event, and performing these rituals allows family members to process their grief. It offers a sense

of closure and allows individuals to say goodbye in a meaningful way.

4. **To Bring Peace to the Family**: These rituals are believed to not only provide peace to the soul of the deceased but also to the family members. It is believed that performing the rituals with faith and sincerity can remove any negative energy or lingering grief from the family, creating a sense of emotional healing.

5. **To Fulfill the Duties of Dharma**: In Hindu tradition, performing rituals for the deceased is considered part of the dharma, the righteous duties of the living. This includes offering prayers and making offerings to ensure that the deceased's soul is guided toward liberation and peace.

Key Post-Death Rituals

The post-death rituals may vary according to different Hindu traditions, regions, and communities. However, the following are the most common rituals performed:

1. **Antyesti (Funeral Ceremony)**:

   The first and foremost ritual is the funeral, called **Antyesti**. It is the last rite that is performed for the deceased to ensure the soul's peaceful transition. The body is typically bathed, dressed in clean clothes, and placed on a bier. Family members then offer their final respects before the body is taken for cremation. The fire used for cremation is said to purify the soul and assist it in the journey to the afterlife.

2. **Cremation and Immersion of Ashes**:

   Cremation is believed to release the soul from its earthly form and allow it to transition to its next stage. After the cremation, the ashes of the deceased are typically immersed in a river, ideally the Ganges. The immersion of ashes signifies the final release of the physical body and the soul's journey onward.

3. **Shraddha (Ritual Offering to Ancestors):**

   Shraddha is a sacred offering made by the family members to the ancestors, performed typically on the 11th day or the 13th day after death, as well as on certain anniversaries of the deceased. The family offers food, water, and other items to the departed soul, and the ritual is believed to help in the journey toward peace and liberation.

4. **Pind Daan (Offering of Rice Balls):**

   This ritual involves offering rice balls (pind) to the soul of the deceased. It is believed that the rice balls represent the physical body, and offering them provides sustenance to the soul. This ritual is often performed during the annual death anniversary or on specific auspicious occasions. It is an act of remembrance, and it is believed to assist the soul in its journey to the afterlife.

5. **Tarpan (Water Offering):**

   Tarpan is a ritual offering of water to the ancestors, performed by the family members. It is done as a mark of respect to the ancestors and to invoke blessings for the well-being of the living family members. The water offering is meant to soothe the departed souls and provide them with peace. Tarpan is typically performed on specific days following the death, including the **Pitr Paksha** (the period of the ancestors) and on the deceased's death anniversary.

6. **Ekodishta (The One-Year Ritual):**

   A key milestone in the post-death rituals is the **Ekodishta**, which takes place after the completion of one year following the death. This ritual signifies the final rites for the deceased and involves specific prayers, offerings, and rituals that mark the end of the mourning period.

7. **Moksha (Liberation of the Soul)**:

    One of the ultimate goals of the rituals after death is to help the soul attain **moksha**, which is liberation from the cycle of birth, death, and rebirth. By performing these rituals with sincerity and devotion, it is believed that the soul is freed from any lingering attachments and is able to attain liberation.

The Spiritual and Scientific Significance of Death Rituals

The rituals performed after death not only have a spiritual significance but also a psychological and scientific impact on the family and society:

1. **Psychological Healing**:

Death rituals help the bereaved family members deal with grief. By following the ritualistic process, individuals find a sense of closure, express their feelings, and come to terms with the loss. This structured process facilitates emotional healing, providing comfort during an extremely painful time.

2. **Reaffirmation of Life's Continuity**:

Hindu death rituals emphasize the continuation of life after death, suggesting that the soul moves on to a new phase. This belief offers a sense of peace to family members, assuring them that death is not the end but a transition to the next stage.

3. **Energy Purification**:

Scientifically, it is believed that rituals, especially those involving offerings of water, food, or incense, can create positive vibrations and purify the energy in the environment. The physical act of performing these rituals can help bring a sense of balance and harmony to those involved.

4. **Connection to the Divine**:

The rituals help individuals connect with the divine, reminding them of the transient nature of life and the eternal nature of the soul. These practices reinforce the belief in a higher power that watches over the soul's journey, helping individuals find peace and solace.

Conclusion

The **rituals after death** serve as an essential aspect of the human experience, offering both practical and spiritual guidance. These ceremonies are meant not only to honor the departed but also to help the soul achieve peace, liberation, and ultimate freedom from the cycle of birth and death. These rituals are grounded in an understanding of both the **spiritual energy** of the universe and the **psychological need** for closure and healing for the family left behind. By performing these rituals, we ensure that the soul is guided on its journey, and at the same time, we honor the memory and contributions of the deceased.

Chapter 29:
The Significance of Eclipse in Hindu Tradition

Eclipses have held a profound significance in Hindu tradition for millennia. These celestial events, when the moon or the sun appears to be temporarily obscured, are not just astronomical phenomena but are also deeply embedded in the spiritual and cultural practices of Hindus. Eclipses, both solar and lunar, are seen as auspicious, inauspicious, and transformative, depending on the context in which they occur.

The Celestial Symbolism

In Hinduism, eclipses symbolize the cosmic balance between light and darkness, good and evil, creation and destruction. They are believed to represent moments of transition, where the forces of the universe are in a state of flux. These cosmic events remind people of the cyclical nature of time and the impermanence of all things in the material world.

1. **Solar Eclipse (Surya Grahan)**: A solar eclipse occurs when the moon comes between the earth and the sun, temporarily blocking the sun's light. In Hindu tradition, the solar eclipse is considered a time of upheaval, a period when the divine light is momentarily concealed. The sun, which represents the ultimate source of energy, power, and life, is temporarily overshadowed, and it is believed that during this period, the cosmic forces may cause disturbances in the natural world.

2. **Lunar Eclipse (Chandra Grahan)**: A lunar eclipse occurs when the earth passes between the sun and the moon, casting its shadow on the moon. This is generally seen as a less intense event than a solar eclipse but is still considered significant. Lunar eclipses are often seen as a time for reflection and introspection. The moon, associated with the mind, emotions, and femininity, is believed to be temporarily

overwhelmed by the shadow of the earth, symbolizing the suppression of one's emotions or thoughts.

Mythological Significance

In Hindu mythology, eclipses are often attributed to the actions of powerful deities and mythological figures. The most popular story revolves around the demon **Rahu** and **Ketu**.

- **The Legend of Rahu and Ketu**: According to Hindu mythology, Rahu and Ketu were once celestial beings who tried to deceive the gods and drink the nectar of immortality (amrit) during the churning of the ocean (Samudra Manthan). Rahu and Ketu, disguised as gods, consumed the nectar. However, Lord Vishnu, noticing their deception, severed their heads. Rahu's head became the cause of the solar eclipse, while Ketu's body caused the lunar eclipse. This myth explains the phenomenon of eclipses and why they are considered a time of cosmic imbalance.

Rahu and Ketu are believed to be shadow planets in Vedic astrology, representing the forces of karma and destiny. Their influence is said to cause disruption, especially during eclipses, and can be considered both positive and negative depending on the individual's karma.

Rituals and Practices During Eclipses

Eclipses are considered moments of heightened energy, both positive and negative. They are believed to have spiritual significance, prompting Hindus to perform specific rituals and practices during these events.

1. **Fasting and Prayers**:

During an eclipse, it is common for people to observe fasting and offer prayers to the gods, especially to Lord Vishnu, Lord Shiva, and other deities. The belief is that fasting and praying during the eclipse purifies the body and soul, helping individuals accumulate spiritual merit (punya) while averting negative influences.

2. **Avoiding Consumption of Food**:

It is traditionally believed that food prepared before the eclipse should not be consumed, as the cosmic energies during the eclipse are believed to disrupt the nutritional value of food, making it impure. Many people refrain from eating during the eclipse and wait until after the event has passed to consume their meals.

3. **Taking a Ritual Bath**:

In many Hindu communities, it is considered highly auspicious to take a bath after the eclipse, symbolizing purification of the body and mind. The ritual bath is believed to cleanse one from any negative energies accumulated during the eclipse. In some places, people even travel to holy rivers like the Ganges to take a bath during the eclipse.

4. **Reciting Mantras**:

Chanting powerful mantras during the eclipse is believed to invoke divine protection and blessings. The **Gayatri Mantra** and other purification mantras like the **Mahamrityunjaya Mantra** are commonly recited to seek spiritual upliftment and shield oneself from any adverse effects during the eclipse.

5. **Meditation and Reflection**:

Eclipses are often viewed as ideal times for deep meditation, reflection, and contemplation. Since the eclipse is seen as a time when cosmic energies are in flux, it is considered an opportunity to align oneself spiritually, reflect on one's life, and meditate on higher truths.

The Psychological Impact and Scientific Explanation

While eclipses are primarily seen through a spiritual lens in Hinduism, modern science has provided an explanation of the phenomenon. Eclipses are natural celestial events caused by the alignment of the earth, sun, and moon. The energy fluctuations that some people experience during eclipses could be due to psychological factors, such as heightened awareness, the sense of mystery, and the collective belief in the significance of the event.

6. **Psychological Impact**:

The belief in eclipses as moments of transformation can have a profound psychological impact. People may feel more introspective, more attuned to their emotions, or experience a heightened sense of anxiety or restlessness. The collective belief in the power of eclipses creates a shared environment where people are more likely to reflect deeply on their lives and their spiritual practices.

7. **Scientific Explanation**:

From a scientific perspective, eclipses are nothing more than the moon or the earth casting their shadows on one another. A solar eclipse occurs when the moon passes between the earth and the sun, blocking the sun's light. A lunar eclipse occurs when the earth casts its shadow on the moon. These phenomena are predictable and follow a natural, cyclical pattern, causing no harm to the earth or its inhabitants.

The Eclipse in the Larger Cosmic Scheme

In Hindu tradition, the eclipse is seen as a cosmic reminder of the ever-changing nature of life. The darkening of the sun or moon is symbolic of the shadows of ignorance, desires, and attachments that obstruct the light of wisdom and knowledge. Just as the eclipse is temporary, so too are the obstacles in life, and they eventually pass, revealing clarity, peace, and light once again.

The eclipse, in essence, serves as a moment for pause, reflection, and renewal. It offers a powerful symbol of transformation and the potential for spiritual awakening.

Conclusion

The significance of eclipses in Hindu tradition goes beyond mere celestial events. They are seen as times of spiritual reflection, purification, and transformation. With their deep roots in mythology, rituals, and practices, eclipses continue to hold profound meaning for those who embrace the cosmic and spiritual insights they provide. Whether seen as a time for fasting, prayer, meditation, or simply reflection, the eclipse serves as a reminder of the impermanence of life and the eternal nature of the soul.

Chapter 30:
Significance of Jal Deepak

In Hinduism, the light of a lamp (Deepak) is often symbolic of knowledge, divinity, and the dispelling of darkness. However, the **Jal Deepak**, or water lamp, is a lesser-known but significant practice in the spiritual traditions of Hinduism. The term "Jal Deepak" refers to a lamp that is lit in water, and this practice carries with it profound spiritual and metaphysical meanings. While traditional oil lamps (deepas) are commonly used for daily worship, the **Jal Deepak** holds a special place in certain rituals and is considered a powerful symbol of purity, devotion, and the connection between the earthly and divine realms.

The Ritual of Jal Deepak

The **Jal Deepak** is usually made by filling a small vessel or bowl with water, placing a floating wick, and lighting it. The wick can be made of cotton or a similar material, and the bowl is often placed on a bed of flowers, leaves, or floating lotus petals, creating a serene and aesthetically pleasing atmosphere. Unlike regular oil lamps, where the wick burns through oil to produce light, the **Jal Deepak** uses water as a medium, with the floating wick being ignited by the power of divinity.

The practice of lighting a **Jal Deepak** can be seen during specific festivals, ceremonies, and pujas, particularly when invoking divine blessings for prosperity, purification, or the removal of negative energies.

Symbolism Behind the Jal Deepak

1. **Purification and Cleansing**:
2. In Hinduism, water is considered a symbol of purity and life. It is believed that water can cleanse both the physical and spiritual realms. The **Jal Deepak** combines the sacred

symbolism of fire and water, two essential elements of the natural world. Fire is often viewed as a purifier and a transformative force, while water represents cleansing, nurturing, and flow. The two elements working together in the **Jal Deepak** symbolize the removal of impurities from both the mind and the surroundings.

3. **Spiritual Illumination:**

Lighting the **Jal Deepak** is a way of invoking spiritual light to dispel the darkness of ignorance. In Hindu philosophy, darkness symbolizes ignorance and negative emotions, while light represents knowledge, wisdom, and divine consciousness. Just as the oil lamp is lit to brighten a dark space, the **Jal Deepak** is lit to invite spiritual illumination into one's life. It is said to bring clarity of thought, mindfulness, and an understanding of the higher self.

4. **Balance of Elements:**

The **Jal Deepak** is an extraordinary representation of the harmony between the elements. The fire from the wick symbolizes the element of **Agni** (fire), while the water in which it floats represents **Jala** (water). In Hindu tradition, these elements are essential in the creation of life and the universe. The act of lighting the **Jal Deepak** is a reminder of the balance between the forces of nature and the necessity of respecting and understanding them for a peaceful existence.

5. **Divine Blessings and Protection:**

The **Jal Deepak** is believed to be a way of inviting the blessings of the divine. Whether it is during a personal prayer or a communal ritual, the flame of the water lamp is thought to carry the power to attract divine protection. It is believed that the presence of the **Jal Deepak** offers safety, warding off negative energies and bringing the blessings of the gods into the home.

Spiritual Significance of Water and Fire

1. **Water (Jala):**

Water is one of the five elements in Hindu philosophy, known as the **Pancha Mahabhutas**, and it holds great significance in the ritualistic practices of the faith. It is said to possess the power to cleanse the body, mind, and spirit. Water is also used in various purification rituals, including taking ritual baths and sprinkling water to bless objects or people. The **Jal Deepak**, therefore, symbolizes the importance of water as a medium of spiritual purification and a conduit for divine energies.

2. **Fire (Agni):**

Fire is also one of the **Pancha Mahabhutas** and holds immense spiritual significance in Hinduism. Agni is the god of fire and is revered as a mediator between humans and the gods, as offerings are often made to the fire during yajnas (fire rituals). Fire is seen as a purifier, transforming offerings into ash, and is central to many Hindu ceremonies. In the **Jal Deepak**, the combination of fire and water represents the balance of the opposing forces, creating an equilibrium between purifying and illuminating energies.

Rituals Involving the Jal Deepak

1. **Aarti with Jal Deepak:**

In certain rituals, particularly in temples dedicated to specific deities such as Lord Shiva, Lord Vishnu, and Goddess Durga, **Jal Deepaks** are lit during the aarti (ceremonial prayer). This is done to create a sacred environment and to symbolize the invocation of divine light and purity. The water lamp is often placed on the altar or in front of the deity's idol, offering a visual representation of devotion and surrender.

2. **Festivals and Special Days:**

The **Jal Deepak** is often used during special occasions like **Sharad Purnima, Makar Sankranti**, and other auspicious days.

It is believed that lighting the **Jal Deepak** on such occasions strengthens the connection between the worshipper and the divine, amplifying the effects of prayers and offerings. Some also believe that the **Jal Deepak** is beneficial in times of personal crises or challenges, as it helps bring spiritual relief and positive energies into the home.

3. **Healing and Protection Rituals**:

People who are going through difficult phases of life or suffering from ill health may light a **Jal Deepak** in their homes as part of healing rituals. It is believed to promote physical, mental, and emotional healing by cleansing the surrounding atmosphere and bringing in calming energies. The flame of the water lamp is also considered a source of protection, creating a shield against negative influences.

Psychological and Emotional Benefits

The act of lighting the **Jal Deepak** can have a profound impact on the mind and emotions. The gentle flicker of the flame, reflected on the surface of the water, creates a tranquil and meditative atmosphere. In times of distress, lighting the **Jal Deepak** and watching its soothing flames can help calm the mind, reduce anxiety, and provide a sense of inner peace. It encourages mindfulness and presence, helping individuals focus on their spiritual growth.

The **Jal Deepak** serves as a constant reminder to the practitioner of the impermanence of life and the importance of spiritual growth. It signifies that, despite challenges and obstacles, the light of wisdom and divinity is always available to illuminate the path of righteousness.

Conclusion

The **Jal Deepak** is much more than just a ritualistic object; it is a representation of the harmonious relationship between the elements, the invocation of divine blessings, and a symbol of spiritual illumination and purification. Whether used during specific religious ceremonies or as a personal tool for meditation, the **Jal Deepak** reminds us of the delicate balance between material and spiritual realms. It encourages us to reflect on our inner state, inviting peace, light, and positivity into our lives. The **Jal Deepak** is a beautiful manifestation of the interconnectedness of fire, water, and the divine forces that govern our existence.

Chapter 31:
Science Behind Surya Namaskar

Surya Namaskar, or the Sun Salutation, is one of the most revered and powerful practices in yoga, often performed as a sequence of twelve physical postures and associated with deep spiritual significance. Traditionally performed to honor the Sun (Surya), the source of life and energy, Surya Namaskar is not just a physical exercise; it integrates the mind, body, and spirit. However, beyond its spiritual and cultural significance, Surya Namaskar has profound scientific and physiological benefits that can enhance one's physical and mental health.

1. The Twelve Postures of Surya Namaskar

The Surya Namaskar sequence involves a set of twelve asanas (postures) that flow smoothly into one another. The sequence typically starts with standing in prayer position (Pranamasana) and proceeds through a series of poses, including standing poses, forward bends, lunges, and backbends, before returning to the starting position. These movements are synchronized with breath to create a harmonious flow, improving the mind-body connection.

- **Pranamasana (Prayer Pose)**: This pose helps to center the mind and connect with the breath.

- **Hasta Uttanasana (Raised Arms Pose)**: This stretch extends the arms and opens up the chest.

- **Padahastasana (Hand to Foot Pose)**: This forward bend stretches the spine and hamstrings.

- **Ashwa Sanchalanasana (Equestrian Pose)**: This deep lunge improves flexibility and strengthens the legs.

- **Dandasana (Plank Pose)**: Strengthens the core and arms.

- **Ashtanga Namaskara (Salutation Pose)**: Involves bringing the body close to the ground, strengthening the chest, shoulders, and arms.

- **Bhujangasana (Cobra Pose)**: Opens the chest and stretches the spine.

- **Adho Mukha Svanasana (Downward Dog Pose)**: A full-body stretch that tones muscles and improves blood circulation.

- **Ashwa Sanchalanasana (Equestrian Pose)**: Another lunge to stretch the legs and hips.

- **Padahastasana (Hand to Foot Pose)**: Another forward bend to stretch the spine.

- **Hasta Uttanasana (Raised Arms Pose)**: Stretches the upper body and lungs.

- **Pranamasana (Prayer Pose)**: The sequence concludes with the same posture as the beginning to bring balance.

2. *Physiological Benefits of Surya Namaskar*

Surya Namaskar offers a range of physical benefits that contribute to overall health and well-being. The practice combines strength, flexibility, and balance, and when performed regularly, it can have the following effects:

- **Increases Flexibility**: The forward bends, backbends, and stretches in Surya Namaskar promote flexibility in the spine, hamstrings, and hips. This improves mobility and reduces the risk of injuries.

- **Strengthens Muscles**: The different poses in Surya Namaskar engage multiple muscle groups, such as the arms, legs, core, and back. Holding these poses builds muscular strength, particularly in the upper body and core.

- **Improves Blood Circulation**: The flow of movements combined with synchronized breathing increases blood circulation throughout the body. Poses like the Downward Dog (Adho Mukha Svanasana) help in reversing blood flow, promoting better circulation to the brain, which may improve mental clarity.

- **Boosts Respiratory Health**: Surya Namaskar involves deep and controlled breathing, which enhances lung capacity and improves the efficiency of the respiratory system. The rhythmic breathing practiced during the sequence helps oxygenate the body and detoxify the lungs.

- **Detoxifies the Body**: The deep stretches and inversions in Surya Namaskar help stimulate the lymphatic system, facilitating the removal of toxins from the body. It also aids in digestion and promotes the functioning of the liver and kidneys.

- **Improves Posture**: Regular practice strengthens the core and improves alignment, reducing the risk of poor posture and back pain. It also relieves tension in the back and neck, which is particularly beneficial for people who spend long hours sitting at desks.

3. Mental and Emotional Benefits

While Surya Namaskar is primarily physical, its benefits extend to mental and emotional health as well:

- **Reduces Stress and Anxiety**: Surya Namaskar involves mindful breathing, which triggers the parasympathetic nervous system and calms the body and mind. The focus on breath and movement helps release built-up tension and lowers stress levels.

- **Improves Concentration**: The practice of synchronizing breath with movement helps to train the mind, leading to increased focus and concentration. The repetitive flow of the poses acts as a form of moving meditation, allowing the practitioner to cultivate mental clarity.

- **Enhances Mood**: Physical exercise in general releases endorphins, the "feel-good" hormones, but Surya Namaskar has an additional spiritual and emotional dimension that elevates mood. The connection with the Sun and the practice of gratitude, integral to Surya Namaskar, fosters positivity and a sense of joy.

- **Emotional Balance**: The practice encourages mindfulness and self-awareness, allowing the practitioner to be in the present moment. This leads to emotional stability, as it helps release negative emotions and encourages a balanced perspective.

4. Scientific Explanation of Surya Namaskar's Impact on the Body

Surya Namaskar combines stretching, strength-building, and cardiovascular exercise in a flowing sequence. The series of postures are designed to engage the body in a way that stimulates various organs, glands, and systems.

- **Endocrine System**: The practice stimulates the thyroid, pituitary, and adrenal glands, which regulate various hormones in the body. This hormonal regulation can help improve metabolism, boost energy levels, and balance emotions.

- **Digestive System**: Many of the postures, such as the forward bends and lunges, aid in massaging the internal organs, particularly the stomach and intestines. This promotes better digestion, improves bowel movement, and reduces bloating and indigestion.

- **Cardiovascular System**: The sequence of postures elevates the heart rate, making Surya Namaskar an excellent cardiovascular workout. This helps in improving heart health, enhancing circulation, and regulating blood pressure.

- **Nervous System**: The deep breathing and focus required in Surya Namaskar activate the parasympathetic nervous system, which is responsible for relaxation and rest. This helps reduce stress and anxiety, improving mental health.

5. Surya Namaskar and the Sun

In addition to its scientific benefits, Surya Namaskar has a spiritual and symbolic connection to the Sun, which is revered in Hinduism as the source of life, energy, and vitality. By performing Surya Namaskar, one symbolically honors the Sun and seeks its blessings for health, prosperity, and well-being. It is believed that practicing Surya Namaskar every day helps align one's energy with the cosmic energy of the Sun, bringing balance and harmony into the practitioner's life.

The twelve postures of Surya Namaskar are said to correspond to the twelve months of the year, and the sequence aligns the practitioner with the natural rhythms of the universe. By honoring the Sun in this way, the practitioner experiences a sense of interconnectedness with nature and the cosmos.

Conclusion

Surya Namaskar is not only a physical exercise but a complete practice that integrates body, mind, and spirit. Its numerous benefits extend from physical health improvements to mental clarity, emotional balance, and spiritual growth. The practice is deeply rooted in the ancient traditions of yoga, yet its scientific explanations and positive effects on the body make it a timeless and universally applicable tool for well-being. Whether performed for physical fitness or as a spiritual practice, Surya Namaskar offers a powerful way to align oneself with the natural forces of the universe and achieve a balanced, healthy life.

Chapter 32:
How Does the Digestive System Function as Per Sunrise and Sunset

The human body operates in accordance with the natural rhythms of the environment. Among the various systems in the body, the digestive system is especially influenced by the cycles of the sun. The connection between our digestive processes and the timings of sunrise and sunset is a fascinating blend of ancient wisdom and modern science. Understanding this connection can help us optimize our digestive health and overall well-being.

1. *The Circadian Rhythm and Digestion*

Our body's internal clock, known as the **circadian rhythm**, is influenced by the rising and setting of the sun. This rhythm regulates numerous bodily functions, including sleep, hormone production, body temperature, and digestion. It is an innate biological cycle that aligns itself with the natural day-night cycle.

- **Morning and Digestive Fire (Agni)**: According to Ayurvedic principles, the digestive system is the most efficient during the morning hours. The term **"Agni"**, meaning digestive fire, is used to describe the body's digestive strength. Agni is believed to be at its peak in the morning, soon after sunrise, when the body is well-rested and prepared to digest food effectively. This is the best time for the body to process heavier and more complex meals.

- **Afternoon Digestion**: By midday, as the sun is at its highest point, our digestive capacity reaches its peak. This is considered the time when the body's metabolism is functioning at its maximum efficiency. Therefore, eating a substantial meal around noon is ideal for the digestive system. The body can process food more effectively and efficiently, utilizing nutrients for energy and vitality.

- **Evening and Digestive Slowdown**: As the day begins to wind down and the sun sets, the digestive fire also begins to decrease. The body's energy begins to focus more on preparation for rest and recovery. Eating heavy meals or consuming large quantities of food late in the evening is not recommended, as the digestive system is less active, which can lead to indigestion, bloating, and disturbed sleep.

2. *Optimal Eating Times According to the Sun*

Understanding the link between digestion and the sun's cycle can help us determine the most beneficial times for eating. Aligning your meals with these natural rhythms can promote better digestion, energy levels, and overall health.

- **Sunrise to Midday (6 AM to 12 PM)**: The period after sunrise is considered the best time to consume the first meal of the day. The digestive system is rested and primed to process food, especially light and nutrient-dense meals. Breakfast should ideally be rich in proteins, fruits, and whole grains, which provide the body with energy for the day ahead.

- **Midday (12 PM to 2 PM)**: This is the time when digestion is at its peak. The body's energy is at its highest, and it can process complex meals effectively. Lunch should be the largest meal of the day, containing proteins, vegetables, whole grains, and healthy fats. This allows the body to extract the maximum nutrients and maintain energy levels throughout the day.

- **Evening (6 PM to 8 PM)**: By evening, the digestive system starts to slow down. It's important to eat a lighter dinner, ideally 2-3 hours before bedtime. Meals should be easily digestible and not too heavy. Avoid consuming foods that are rich in fats, sugars, or complex carbohydrates, as they can disrupt digestion and lead to discomfort or indigestion.

- **Late Night (after 8 PM)**: As the sun sets and the body prepares for rest, it's advisable to refrain from eating. The digestive system is in a relaxed state, and consuming food late at night can disrupt sleep patterns, leading to poor-quality sleep and digestion. Late-night eating is also associated with weight gain, as the body is less efficient in metabolizing food at night.

3. The Role of Light and Darkness in Digestion

The digestive system is intricately connected to the cycles of light and darkness. Light exposure, particularly the blue light from the sun, helps regulate the production of important hormones that influence digestion.

- **Light Exposure and Digestive Efficiency**: The bright light of day triggers the production of certain hormones, such as **cortisol**, which increases alertness and helps kickstart the digestive system. The exposure to sunlight in the morning enhances metabolism and the body's ability to digest food efficiently. This is why morning is the ideal time for meals, as the digestive fire (Agni) is at its peak.

- **Darkness and the Parasympathetic Nervous System**: As the day progresses and darkness falls, the production of **melatonin** (the hormone responsible for sleep) increases. The body transitions from the sympathetic state (fight or flight) to the parasympathetic state (rest and digest). During this time, the digestive system is less active, and metabolism begins to slow down. Eating late at night disrupts this process and can lead to digestive issues.

4. Scientific Explanation of the Body's Digestive Cycle

Modern science also supports the ancient wisdom that our digestive system is synchronized with the day-night cycle. Studies have shown that the body's circadian rhythm is regulated by the suprachiasmatic nucleus (SCN) in the hypothalamus, which is sensitive to light. The SCN controls the release of hormones such as cortisol, insulin, and melatonin, which influence digestion and metabolism.

- **Cortisol**: Known as the "stress hormone," cortisol also plays a significant role in regulating metabolism. It peaks in the morning, which helps to prepare the digestive system for food intake. High cortisol levels are associated with increased metabolic activity and appetite.

- **Insulin Sensitivity**: Research has shown that insulin sensitivity is higher during the day, particularly after sunrise and throughout the afternoon. This means the body is more efficient at processing food and storing energy. In the evening, insulin sensitivity decreases, making it harder to process food effectively.

- **Gastrointestinal Motility**: The stomach and intestines have a rhythmic movement pattern, known as peristalsis, which helps move food through the digestive tract. These movements are governed by the circadian rhythm and are more efficient during daylight hours, aligning with our body's natural digestive peak after sunrise and noon.

5. Practical Tips for Healthy Digestion Based on the Sun's Cycle

- **Eat Breakfast Early**: Start your day with a healthy, balanced breakfast soon after sunrise. Include fruits, whole grains, and protein-rich foods to fuel your body.

- **Have a Substantial Lunch**: Aim to have your largest meal at noon or early afternoon, when your digestive system is at its best. Include a variety of nutrient-dense foods such as vegetables, lean proteins, and whole grains.

- **Avoid Heavy Meals at Night**: Keep your dinner light and easily digestible. Opt for lighter options like soups, salads, and steamed vegetables that will not overwhelm the digestive system before bedtime.

- **Limit Late-Night Snacking**: Refrain from eating heavy meals or snacks late at night. The digestive system is not designed to process food effectively during the evening, so eating late can disrupt digestion and interfere with your sleep.

Conclusion

The body's digestive system functions most effectively when it is in sync with the natural rhythms of sunrise and sunset. By aligning our eating patterns with these rhythms, we can optimize digestion, improve metabolism, and support overall health. The ancient wisdom that links the digestive process with the cycles of the sun is not only spiritually significant but also scientifically sound, offering us a simple yet powerful way to enhance our well-being through mindful eating and respect for nature's cycles.

Chapter 33:
Science Behind Drinking Water Energized in Different Coloured Bottles

Water is often considered the essence of life, not only sustaining our physical health but also influencing our mental and emotional well-being. Over the years, various traditions and alternative healing practices have emphasized the significance of water, not just for its hydration properties but for its energetic potential. One such practice involves drinking water that has been stored in bottles of different colors. Many believe that water, when kept in colored containers, absorbs energy from the color, potentially enhancing the drinker's health and vitality. But is there any scientific basis behind this idea?

In this chapter, we explore the concept of energized water and how different colored bottles are said to influence its properties. From ancient traditions to modern scientific studies, we delve into how the colors of the bottles might affect water and the human body.

1. The Influence of Color on Water

Colors are a fundamental part of our environment and have long been known to affect our mood, energy, and physical health. This is rooted in the science of **chromotherapy**, or color therapy, which is based on the idea that different colors correspond to different wavelengths of light. Each wavelength of light carries a specific amount of energy, and when applied to the body, it is believed to influence various physiological and psychological states.

Water, being a universal solvent, is sensitive to environmental influences, including light and color. The theory behind using different colored bottles for storing and drinking water is that the water absorbs the energy or vibrations associated with that color. The absorbed energy is then thought to be transferred to the body when consumed.

2. *The Impact of Each Color*

Let's explore the impact of some common colors and how they are believed to energize water:

- **Red Bottles: Stimulation and Vitality** Red is a color that represents energy, power, and passion. It is often associated with stimulating the body, increasing circulation, and enhancing vitality. Drinking water stored in red-colored bottles is believed to help invigorate the body and mind, making it an ideal choice for individuals who are feeling lethargic or low on energy. Red is thought to promote heat, so it is often recommended in colder climates to warm the body and increase alertness.

- **Blue Bottles: Calmness and Mental Clarity** Blue is known for its calming properties and is often associated with tranquility, peace, and mental clarity. It is believed that drinking water from blue-colored bottles can help reduce stress and anxiety, promoting a sense of calmness. The color blue is also linked to the throat chakra in many healing traditions, which governs communication and expression. Drinking blue-energized water is thought to support clear thinking and better communication skills.

- **Green Bottles: Healing and Balance** Green is a color often associated with nature, growth, and healing. It is said to possess soothing and balancing properties that can promote physical and emotional healing. Green is also connected to the heart chakra, which governs love, compassion, and emotional well-being. Drinking water stored in green-colored bottles is believed to promote healing, restore balance, and reduce feelings of negativity or emotional turmoil.

- **Yellow Bottles: Energy and Positivity** Yellow represents positivity, happiness, and intellectual energy. It is thought to stimulate mental clarity, enhance concentration, and uplift the mood. Water stored in yellow-colored bottles is believed to enhance cognitive function and stimulate the solar plexus chakra, which is associated with self-confidence and personal power. It is said to be particularly beneficial for those who are feeling mentally fatigued or lacking in motivation.

- **Orange Bottles: Creativity and Joy** Orange is the color of creativity, joy, and enthusiasm. It is thought to stimulate the sacral chakra, which governs creativity, sexuality, and emotional expression. Drinking water from orange-colored bottles is believed to help boost creativity, encourage a positive outlook, and enhance one's ability to express themselves. It is often recommended for individuals seeking emotional release or looking to overcome creative blocks.

- **Pink Bottles: Love and Emotional Healing** Pink is the color of love, compassion, and emotional healing. It is linked to the heart chakra and is believed to have a calming and nurturing effect on the emotions. Drinking water from pink-colored bottles is thought to promote feelings of love, compassion, and self-care. It is also believed to be helpful in reducing emotional stress and healing emotional wounds, making it ideal for individuals going through difficult emotional times.

- **Purple Bottles: Spiritual Awareness and Intuition** Purple, often associated with spirituality and intuition, is believed to help elevate one's consciousness. It is said to stimulate the third eye chakra, which governs intuition, psychic abilities, and spiritual awareness. Drinking water from purple-colored bottles is thought to enhance spiritual insight, improve meditation practices, and promote a sense of connection to the divine.

- **Clear Bottles: Purity and Neutral Energy** Clear bottles are often used as neutral containers, as they do not carry any specific energetic influence. The water stored in clear bottles is believed to maintain its natural, unaltered state. Some people prefer using clear bottles for this reason, especially those who want to maintain the purity of the water without introducing any specific energetic vibrations. Clear bottles are often considered ideal for hydration in everyday life.

3. The Role of Crystals and Water

In addition to colored bottles, another popular practice is to use **crystals** to energize water. Many believe that certain crystals can be placed in the water to enhance its vibrational qualities. For example, placing **rose quartz** in a water bottle is thought to infuse the water with loving energy, while **amethyst** is used to promote calmness and spiritual awareness. When combined with colored bottles, crystals are believed to further amplify the energy of the water.

4. Scientific Perspective: Water's Memory and Vibrational Energy

From a scientific standpoint, water has a unique property: **water's memory**. This concept suggests that water can retain information or energy that it comes into contact with. While this idea is still under investigation, research by **Dr. Masaru Emoto** has demonstrated that water molecules can form different crystalline structures based on the type of energy or intention they are exposed to. In his studies, water exposed to positive emotions, words, or music formed beautiful and symmetrical crystals, whereas water exposed to negative influences formed distorted, irregular crystals.

While the link between water and color energy is not yet fully established by mainstream science, there is growing interest in exploring the vibrational properties of water. Studies in quantum physics and energy fields suggest that different colors and frequencies of light can influence water at a molecular level, potentially enhancing its healing properties.

5. Practical Tips for Using Colored Water Bottles

- **Choose a color based on your needs**: If you are feeling mentally tired, a yellow or orange bottle might help boost your mood and creativity. If you're looking for peace and tranquility, a blue or green bottle could be the ideal choice.

- **Experiment with different colors**: If you're curious, try using water stored in bottles of different colors for a period of time and observe how it affects your physical and emotional state. Each person may have a different response to color energies.

- **Combine with other practices**: For even greater benefits, you can combine drinking energized water with other holistic practices like meditation, yoga, or mindfulness. The power of intention and belief also plays a significant role in amplifying the effects of energized water.

Conclusion

While the idea of drinking water from colored bottles may seem unconventional, it is rooted in the belief that water, as a powerful medium of energy, can absorb and transmit the energetic qualities of different colors. Whether or not you fully believe in the energetic properties of water, there is no doubt that color can have a psychological and emotional impact on us, influencing our mood, energy, and well-being. By understanding the science behind color and water, you can use these practices to support your physical, mental, and emotional health.

Chapter 34:
Mitahar (Balanced Diet)

In the realm of health and wellness, the concept of a **balanced diet** or **Mitahar** holds great importance. "Mitahar," derived from the Sanskrit words **'Mita'** (moderate) and **'Ahara'** (food), is a traditional approach to eating that emphasizes moderation, balance, and the nourishment of both the body and the mind. In Hindu philosophy, dietary practices are not just about satisfying hunger; they are deeply connected to one's spiritual and emotional well-being. The principle of Mitahar is rooted in the belief that food is not only essential for physical sustenance but also plays a significant role in maintaining mental clarity and spiritual peace.

In this chapter, we explore the meaning and significance of Mitahar, its practical implementation in daily life, and its relevance in contemporary health practices. We also delve into how a balanced diet is crucial for maintaining overall health, longevity, and well-being.

1. The Concept of Mitahar

Mitahar is more than just eating the right types of food; it is about **mindful eating** and making conscious choices regarding what, when, and how we eat. In ancient texts like the **Ayurveda**, the focus is on the quality, quantity, and timing of food, which are all key elements of maintaining harmony in the body and mind.

The idea of Mitahar revolves around three main aspects:

- **Moderation**: Eating in moderation ensures that we do not overindulge or deprive ourselves of essential nutrients. Overeating leads to lethargy and digestive problems, while under-eating can cause nutritional deficiencies and low energy levels.

- **Variety**: A balanced diet is one that includes a wide variety of foods that provide essential nutrients, vitamins, minerals, and antioxidants. Eating a wide range of foods helps support the body's many functions and promotes overall health.

- **Consciousness and Connection**: Eating with awareness and gratitude connects us to the food we consume. It's about appreciating the source of food, understanding its effects on the body, and developing a relationship with food that nourishes not only the body but also the soul.

2. The Role of Ayurveda in Mitahar

In **Ayurveda**, the traditional Indian system of medicine, food is categorized based on its effects on the body and mind. According to Ayurveda, every individual has a unique constitution, known as **Prakriti**, and a balanced diet should be tailored to that constitution. The three primary energies, or **Doshas—Vata**, **Pitta**, and **Kapha**—play a vital role in determining the right kind of food for each person.

- **Vata** types are generally light, dry, and airy. They are encouraged to consume warm, moist, and grounding foods such as soups, stews, and cooked grains.

- **Pitta** types are fiery and intense. They are advised to eat cooling, hydrating foods such as cucumbers, melons, dairy products, and leafy greens.

- **Kapha** types are heavy and slow. They benefit from light, stimulating foods such as spicy dishes, legumes, and grains like barley, oats, and quinoa.

By understanding one's Dosha, one can create a diet that not only provides nourishment but also helps maintain harmony within the body.

3. The Key Components of a Balanced Diet (Mitahar)

A well-balanced diet, as advocated by Mitahar, consists of the following:

- **Carbohydrates**: Carbs provide energy and are an essential part of a balanced diet. Whole grains like rice, wheat, barley, and millets, as well as root vegetables like sweet potatoes, offer slow-releasing energy and are rich in fiber.

- **Proteins**: Proteins are essential for muscle repair, growth, and immune function. Vegetarian sources of protein include lentils, chickpeas, tofu, paneer, and dairy products, while non-vegetarian sources include eggs, fish, and chicken.

- **Fats**: Healthy fats are essential for the body's cell structure, hormone production, and brain health. Sources of good fats include nuts, seeds, avocados, olive oil, ghee, and fatty fish like salmon.

- **Fruits and Vegetables**: These provide essential vitamins, minerals, antioxidants, and dietary fiber. Seasonal and local produce are often recommended for their higher nutrient content and connection to nature's rhythm.

- **Spices and Herbs**: Spices like turmeric, ginger, cumin, coriander, and fennel not only enhance flavor but also have medicinal properties. In Ayurveda, certain spices are believed to aid digestion and balance the Doshas. For example, **turmeric** is known for its anti-inflammatory properties, and **cumin** helps in digestion.

- **Water**: Proper hydration is crucial for digestion, detoxification, and overall health. According to Ayurvedic principles, drinking warm water with a pinch of salt or lemon in the morning can help activate the digestive fire (**Agni**) and promote better digestion throughout the day.

4. The Importance of Eating According to Nature's Rhythms

Mitahar stresses the importance of eating according to nature's rhythms. **Ayurveda** emphasizes the connection between the body and nature, suggesting that food should be consumed in alignment with the body's internal clock and the external environment. For example, eating large meals late at night or too close to bedtime can disrupt digestion, leading to issues such as acidity, bloating, and weight gain.

- **Morning**: The morning is the best time to consume food, especially grains and proteins, as the digestive fire is strongest at this time. A nutritious breakfast is key to jump-starting metabolism for the day.

- **Afternoon**: The mid-day is the time when the digestive fire is at its peak, so it is the ideal time for the largest meal of the day. A balanced lunch consisting of carbohydrates, proteins, vegetables, and healthy fats supports sustained energy throughout the afternoon.

- **Evening**: The evening should consist of a lighter meal that is easy to digest. Avoiding heavy or spicy foods before bedtime can help ensure better sleep quality.

5. Mindful Eating: The Practice of Eating with Awareness

A key aspect of Mitahar is **mindful eating**. Mindful eating involves paying full attention to the eating process, from preparing the food to savoring each bite. It encourages individuals to slow down, be present in the moment, and connect with the food they are eating. This practice not only promotes better digestion but also helps foster a deeper sense of gratitude for the food that nourishes the body.

Mindful eating has been linked to improved digestion, weight management, and emotional well-being. It encourages eating without distractions such as television or phones, allowing the mind to focus on the sensory experience of food.

6. The Spiritual Aspect of Mitahar

In Hinduism, food is viewed not just as sustenance but as a form of **prasad** (blessed offering). It is believed that the food we consume directly impacts our mental, physical, and spiritual state. A balanced diet, according to Mitahar, is not just about filling the stomach but also about purifying the body and mind, thereby bringing us closer to spiritual enlightenment.

When food is prepared with love, devotion, and care, it is thought to elevate our consciousness. The process of cooking and eating becomes an act of offering to the divine, transforming a simple meal into a sacred ritual.

7. Practical Tips for Implementing Mitahar in Daily Life

- **Balance your meals**: Aim for a variety of foods in every meal to ensure that you get the right combination of nutrients. This will support your overall health and energy levels.

- **Eat seasonally and locally**: Choose foods that are in season and grown locally. These foods tend to be fresher, more nutrient-dense, and environmentally sustainable.

- **Practice portion control**: Avoid overeating by paying attention to portion sizes. Eating in moderation is key to maintaining a healthy weight and promoting better digestion.

- **Avoid distractions**: Make mealtime a sacred time to connect with your food. Eat without distractions like phones or television to promote mindful eating.

- **Drink water mindfully**: Drink water throughout the day to stay hydrated, but avoid drinking large amounts during meals, as it may dilute digestive juices.

Conclusion

Mitahar, or the practice of eating a balanced and mindful diet, is an essential principle in Hindu philosophy and Ayurvedic medicine. By emphasizing moderation, variety, and conscious eating, Mitahar promotes not just physical health but also mental and spiritual well-being. Implementing Mitahar in daily life encourages a deeper connection to the food we eat, fostering gratitude and respect for the nourishment it provides. Through a balanced diet, we can maintain harmony within our bodies and minds, supporting a life of health, happiness, and spiritual growth.

Chapter 35:
Science of Touching Feet to Take Blessings

In many cultures, particularly in Hinduism, **touching feet** as a gesture of respect and seeking blessings is an age-old tradition. This practice is not merely a symbolic or ritualistic gesture but is rooted in deep cultural, psychological, and scientific significance. In this chapter, we will explore the science behind why touching feet for blessings is considered so powerful and how it positively impacts the body, mind, and spirit.

1. *The Spiritual and Cultural Significance*

In Hindu tradition, **touching the feet** of elders, teachers, or spiritual leaders is a sign of humility, respect, and gratitude. It is believed to invoke divine blessings and wisdom. The feet are regarded as the most sacred part of the body because they represent the foundation of a person's life and journey. By touching the feet of a revered person, one is symbolically honoring their knowledge, wisdom, and spiritual stature.

In spiritual texts like the **Upanishads** and the **Puranas**, the feet are often depicted as the foundation of spiritual power and grace. The act of bowing or touching the feet is not only a show of respect but also a way of aligning oneself with the divine energy that the feet represent.

2. *The Connection Between Feet and Energy Centers*

The feet, especially the soles, contain numerous **nerve endings** and are connected to vital energy points in the body. In **reflexology**, the feet are considered a map of the body, with specific points corresponding to organs, muscles, and other parts of the body. When a person touches the feet of someone else, they are, in a sense, coming into contact with these powerful energy centers.

The Science Behind the Gesture:

- **Acupressure Points**: The soles of the feet are home to several important acupressure points that are believed to correspond to the body's organs. When you touch the feet of another person, the body's energy system interacts with these points, transferring beneficial energy. This physical contact can help activate these points and stimulate the flow of energy throughout the body.

- **Nerve Endings**: The feet have a rich network of nerve endings that can affect the entire body when stimulated. By touching the feet, you are engaging with these sensitive nerve endings. This physical interaction may trigger a release of endorphins, which are the body's natural painkillers, resulting in a sense of calmness and relaxation.

- **Grounding Energy**: In **energy healing practices**, it is believed that the feet connect us to the **earth's electromagnetic field**, a phenomenon known as **grounding**. When we touch the feet of an elder or a revered figure, the energy exchange that occurs can act as a balancing force, helping to restore harmony to our mind and body. The earth's energy is grounding and stabilizing, and through this gesture, we may absorb this stabilizing energy.

3. Psychological and Emotional Impact

While the act of touching feet is rooted in ancient traditions, its psychological impact is profound. The **mind-body connection** is integral to our emotional well-being, and engaging in rituals like touching feet can have a calming effect on the nervous system.

- **Humility and Respect**: The act of touching feet is a humble acknowledgment of someone's superior knowledge, wisdom, or spiritual stature. It places the person in a position of **humility**, which can help lower stress levels and encourage emotional release. Humility is often associated with reduced feelings of ego, which allows a person to be more open, calm, and receptive to spiritual energy and blessings.

- **Psychological Healing**: In many cultures, elders or spiritual guides are seen as **mental and emotional anchors**. Their blessings can offer comfort and peace. Touching their feet is not just about receiving blessings but also about grounding oneself emotionally. It allows the person seeking blessings to feel **reassured** and supported, helping to heal emotional wounds.

- **Fostering Connection**: The touch of feet represents a deep **connection** with another person on a personal and spiritual level. It strengthens relationships and cultivates a sense of belonging and care, which plays an important role in mental well-being.

4. The Power of Blessings

In many spiritual practices, blessings are considered potent forms of energy that have the power to uplift, heal, and guide individuals. When we seek blessings from elders or spiritual figures, it is believed that we are receiving an energy transmission that helps align us with higher consciousness, better decision-making, and spiritual wisdom.

- **Vibration of Blessings**: Blessings are not merely words but are believed to carry a certain **vibration** or frequency. The act of touching feet is considered an energetic exchange between the seeker and the giver of blessings. This exchange creates a bond and allows the seeker to absorb the positive energy from the elder or spiritual guide.

- **Chakra Alignment**: In **yoga** and **meditation** practices, it is believed that human beings have multiple energy centers called **chakras**, which govern different aspects of our physical, emotional, and spiritual health. The **root chakra** located at the base of the spine, and the **crown chakra**, located at the top of the head, are two of the primary energy points in the body. The feet are connected to the root chakra, which governs stability, safety, and grounding. Touching the feet of an elder can help align this chakra and, by extension, bring greater balance and harmony to one's life.

- **The Energy of Blessings**: In the act of offering blessings, there is an exchange of divine energy between the giver and the receiver. The giver transmits their wisdom, compassion, and positive energy to the one seeking blessings. By touching the feet, the seeker aligns themselves with the high vibrations of the giver's wisdom, allowing the energy to flow into their own system. This transfer of positive energy helps the seeker gain clarity, strength, and peace of mind.

5. The Importance of Rituals in Modern Times

In today's fast-paced, technology-driven world, many rituals like touching feet might be seen as old-fashioned or unnecessary. However, the scientific, psychological, and spiritual significance of these practices cannot be overstated. These rituals, especially when practiced with sincerity, have the power to reconnect us with our roots, provide comfort, and restore balance in our lives.

- **Calming Effect**: In times of stress or emotional turmoil, participating in rituals like touching the feet of an elder can serve as an emotional anchor, providing comfort and a sense of reassurance.

- **Strengthening Traditions**: Practicing rituals that honor elders, parents, and teachers helps preserve cultural values and reinforces the importance of respect, gratitude, and humility in society. It strengthens social bonds and fosters a sense of unity and community.

Conclusion

Touching feet to take blessings is not merely a symbolic act but one that carries deep psychological, physiological, and spiritual significance. This gesture allows for an exchange of energy, promotes emotional healing, and helps us align with higher wisdom and consciousness. Whether for the sake of respect, humility, or spiritual growth, the science of touching feet shows how deeply connected our body, mind, and soul are, and how rituals can serve as powerful tools for personal transformation. By engaging in such practices with sincerity, we can tap into the ancient wisdom that has been passed down through generations and continue to benefit from the blessings that come our way.

Chapter 36:
Anulom Vilom and Nadi Shodhan

In the world of yoga and pranayama, **Anulom Vilom** and **Nadi Shodhan** are two powerful breathing techniques that have been practiced for centuries. These techniques are designed to purify the mind and body, and they play a crucial role in maintaining optimal health and well-being. In this chapter, we will explore the significance, the scientific benefits, and the step-by-step process of Anulom Vilom and Nadi Shodhan, and how these practices can help balance and align the body's energy channels.

1. *What is Anulom Vilom?*

Anulom Vilom, also known as **Nadi Shodhan Pranayama** (the "alternate nostril breathing" technique), is one of the most powerful breathing exercises in yoga. It involves inhaling and exhaling alternately through each nostril, with the other nostril blocked. This practice helps to balance the **left and right hemispheres of the brain**, calm the mind, reduce stress, and improve overall respiratory function.

- **Anulom**: The word "Anulom" means "with the grain" or "in the natural way," which refers to the natural, smooth inhalation through the nostrils.

- **Vilom**: "Vilom" means "against the grain," which refers to exhalation through the nostrils with the opposite hand blocking one of them.

2. *What is Nadi Shodhan?*

Nadi Shodhan, also known as **Nadi Cleansing**, is another name for the Anulom Vilom technique. "Nadi" refers to the energy channels through which prana (life force) flows in the body, and "Shodhan" means "purification" or "cleansing." This practice purifies these nadis (energy channels), which are responsible for the smooth flow of prana throughout the body.

The Nadi Shodhan technique involves the alternate breathing process through both nostrils, which is said to help clear blockages in the energy channels. It is believed to balance the **Ida** and **Pingala** nadis, which correspond to the left and right sides of the body, respectively.

- **Ida Nadi**: The left channel, associated with the lunar energy, represents calmness, intuition, and emotional balance.
- **Pingala Nadi**: The right channel, associated with the solar energy, represents action, vitality, and strength.

Balancing these two energies through Nadi Shodhan is thought to help promote mental clarity, emotional stability, and physical health.

3. The Benefits of Anulom Vilom and Nadi Shodhan

Both Anulom Vilom and Nadi Shodhan offer numerous benefits that positively impact the body, mind, and spirit. Some of the key benefits include:

Physical Benefits:

- **Improved Oxygen Intake**: The practice of alternate nostril breathing helps to increase lung capacity and improves oxygen supply to the body. This can result in enhanced stamina, better cardiovascular health, and stronger respiratory function.
- **Detoxification**: By cleansing the energy channels (nadis), Anulom Vilom helps to remove toxins from the body, improving detoxification and promoting better blood circulation.
- **Balanced Blood Pressure**: Studies have shown that Nadi Shodhan can help regulate blood pressure. It calms the

nervous system and reduces hypertension by promoting a state of relaxation.

- **Better Digestion**: This practice has been linked to improved digestive health due to the relaxation of the nervous system, leading to a better-functioning digestive system.

Mental and Emotional Benefits:

- **Stress Relief**: One of the most significant benefits of Anulom Vilom and Nadi Shodhan is stress reduction. By calming the nervous system, it helps to reduce anxiety, depression, and mental fatigue, bringing the mind into a state of peace and relaxation.

- **Improved Focus and Clarity**: The balancing of the left and right hemispheres of the brain promotes mental clarity, sharper concentration, and enhanced focus. This is especially beneficial for individuals looking to improve their productivity, decision-making, and memory.

- **Emotional Stability**: Practicing Nadi Shodhan helps balance the Ida and Pingala nadis, which regulate emotions. This results in better emotional stability, reduced mood swings, and improved mental health.

Spiritual Benefits:

- **Increased Awareness and Mindfulness**: Anulom Vilom helps increase awareness of the present moment, creating a sense of mindfulness and spiritual awakening. The practice of alternate nostril breathing can lead to enhanced spiritual growth by improving meditation and enhancing the connection to one's inner self.

- **Cleansing of Energy Channels**: As Nadi Shodhan purifies the nadis, it is believed to lead to the flow of prana (life energy) throughout the body. This increased energy flow helps maintain balance and vitality, leading to a deeper sense of spiritual well-being.

- **Enhanced Meditation**: Anulom Vilom serves as a preparatory technique for deeper meditation. By calming the mind and improving focus, it makes meditation more effective and fulfilling.

4. Step-by-Step Guide to Practicing Anulom Vilom and Nadi Shodhan

Here is a simple step-by-step guide to performing Anulom Vilom or Nadi Shodhan:

1. **Find a Comfortable Seat**: Sit in a comfortable and relaxed position with your back straight. You can sit in Sukhasana (easy pose) or Padmasana (lotus pose) on a mat or chair.

2. **Rest Your Hands**: Place your hands on your knees with your palms facing upwards in a relaxed position. Use your right hand for the pranayama practice (use the **Vishnu mudra** with the thumb and ring finger to block the nostrils).

3. **Close the Right Nostril**: Using your right thumb, gently close your right nostril. Breathe in deeply and slowly through your left nostril.

4. **Close the Left Nostril**: After inhaling, close your left nostril with your right ring finger, and then open your right nostril.

5. **Exhale Through the Right Nostril**: Exhale slowly and completely through the right nostril.

6. **Inhale Through the Right Nostril**: Inhale deeply through the right nostril.

7. **Close the Right Nostril**: Close the right nostril with the right thumb, and then open the left nostril.

8. **Exhale Through the Left Nostril**: Exhale slowly and completely through the left nostril.

9. **Continue the Cycle**: Repeat this process for 10 to 20 minutes, focusing on smooth, controlled, and rhythmic breathing.

Tips for Practice:

- Perform this practice on an empty stomach or at least two to three hours after a meal.
- Ensure that you are breathing deeply from your diaphragm, not just your chest.
- Practice in a quiet, calm environment free from distractions.
- Always listen to your body. If you feel dizzy or uncomfortable, stop and resume when you feel ready.

5. Conclusion

Anulom Vilom and Nadi Shodhan are transformative practices that offer a wide range of physical, mental, emotional, and spiritual benefits. By incorporating these techniques into your daily routine, you can experience improved respiratory health, reduced stress levels, emotional stability, enhanced mental clarity, and spiritual growth. These practices not only purify the body's energy channels but also help you align with your higher self, leading to a harmonious and balanced life. Whether you're new to yoga or an experienced practitioner, Anulom Vilom and Nadi Shodhan are invaluable tools for fostering overall well-being and achieving inner peace.

Chapter 37:
Tratak Kriya

In the realm of yoga and meditation, **Tratak Kriya** is one of the most profound and effective practices for improving concentration, mental clarity, and inner peace. This practice involves focused gazing, and it has been utilized for centuries as a tool to sharpen the mind, enhance mindfulness, and awaken spiritual energy. In this chapter, we will explore the significance, benefits, and technique of **Tratak Kriya**, as well as its impact on physical, mental, and spiritual health.

1. What is Tratak Kriya?

Tratak Kriya is a yogic technique that involves focusing one's gaze on a single point or object, without blinking, to enhance concentration and purify the mind. The word "Tratak" comes from the Sanskrit term "Trataka," which means "to gaze" or "to look intently." In Tratak, the practitioner focuses on a point of attention, which could be a flame, a candle, a dot, or even an image, while maintaining a steady and unwavering gaze. The eyes are the windows to the soul, and this practice is designed to cleanse both the eyes and the mind, promoting clarity, focus, and calmness.

2. Types of Tratak Kriya

Tratak Kriya can be practiced in various forms, depending on the object of focus:

1. **Candle Tratak (Dīpa Tratak):** This is the most common form of Tratak, where the practitioner gazes at the flame of a candle. The candle flame symbolizes light and purity, and this practice helps sharpen the mind and enhance concentration.

2. **Dot Tratak**: In this form, the practitioner focuses on a small dot or an object such as a black dot drawn on paper or a small symbol. This form is typically used for improving mental focus and training the mind to stay concentrated.

3. **Image Tratak (Murti Tratak)**: In this form, the practitioner gazes at a deity's image, a photograph, or a picture of a spiritual figure. This method is commonly used for meditation and connecting with higher consciousness.

4. **Kundalini Tratak**: This advanced technique involves gazing at a specific point on the forehead or a particular point of concentration in the body to stimulate the **Kundalini energy**. It is said to help awaken higher spiritual awareness.

3. The Science Behind Tratak Kriya

Tratak Kriya involves intense focus and controlled concentration, which leads to a series of physiological and psychological benefits. Some of the significant scientific reasons behind the effectiveness of Tratak Kriya are:

- **Improves Eye Health**: One of the major benefits of Tratak Kriya is that it strengthens the eye muscles and improves overall eye health. By practicing Tratak, the eye muscles are exercised and toned, reducing strain and increasing eye coordination. It also helps in treating conditions like **astigmatism** and **nearsightedness**.

- **Increases Mental Clarity**: The practice of gazing at a single point helps eliminate distractions and calms the mind. It increases the flow of energy to the **pineal gland**, which regulates the production of melatonin and enhances mental clarity. Over time, this practice can significantly improve concentration, focus, and memory.

- **Reduces Stress and Anxiety**: Tratak helps in reducing the constant chatter of the mind and brings the practitioner into the present moment. The focused gaze helps in calming the nervous system, reducing anxiety, and promoting relaxation. It is an excellent practice for managing stress and emotional turmoil.

- **Balances the Nervous System**: Tratak Kriya stimulates the **autonomic nervous system**, leading to better regulation of the body's functions, such as heart rate and blood pressure. The relaxation response activated by Tratak is beneficial for overall well-being and emotional stability.
- **Enhances Meditation and Spiritual Awareness**: By focusing on a single object or point, the practitioner enters a state of deep meditation. This practice is said to help in activating the **third eye** or **Ajna chakra**, leading to heightened intuition, greater spiritual awareness, and a deeper connection with the inner self.

4. Benefits of Tratak Kriya

Tratak Kriya offers a variety of physical, mental, and spiritual benefits, making it a valuable practice in the realm of yoga and self-improvement. Some of the key benefits include:

Physical Benefits:

- Improves vision and strengthens eye muscles.
- Reduces eye strain and fatigue.
- Enhances concentration and mental clarity.
- Balances and calms the nervous system.
- Improves blood circulation and energy flow in the body.

Mental Benefits:

- Reduces stress and anxiety by calming the mind.
- Increases mental clarity and focus.
- Improves memory, attention span, and learning ability.

- Enhances emotional stability and reduces mental exhaustion.
- Promotes a sense of mental peace and relaxation.

Spiritual Benefits:

- Enhances meditation and mindfulness.
- Activates the **Ajna chakra**, leading to greater intuition and self-awareness.
- Promotes spiritual awakening and higher consciousness.
- Strengthens the connection with the divine or higher self.

5. Step-by-Step Guide to Practicing Tratak Kriya

Here is a simple guide on how to practice Tratak Kriya:

1. **Choose a Comfortable Seat**: Sit in a comfortable position with your spine straight and your body relaxed. You can sit in **Sukhasana** (easy pose), **Padmasana** (lotus pose), or any seated position that feels comfortable.

2. **Prepare the Object of Focus**: Place a lit candle in front of you at eye level, about three feet away. The flame should be steady and not flickering. If you are using a dot or image, ensure it is positioned at eye level as well.

3. **Focus Your Gaze**: Begin by gazing at the flame or object without blinking. Try to focus your attention on the center of the flame or the dot. If your eyes start to water, do not wipe them. Simply continue focusing with a relaxed and calm mind.

4. **Breathe Slowly and Deeply**: While gazing at the object, breathe in slowly and deeply through your nostrils. Focus on the breath and the object you are gazing at. Inhale deeply through your abdomen, and exhale gently through your nose.

5. **Maintain Focus**: Continue focusing on the flame, dot, or image for as long as you can without blinking. Beginners may find it difficult to maintain focus for long, but gradually, with practice, the duration will increase. Aim for at least 5–10 minutes of practice.

6. **Close Your Eyes**: After some time, gently close your eyes. Focus on the afterimage of the flame or object in your mind's eye. This helps strengthen the power of concentration and allows your mind to settle into a meditative state.

7. **Repeat the Process**: Open your eyes and repeat the process. Focus on the object again, and after a few minutes, close your eyes to visualize the afterimage. Repeat this process for about 10–15 minutes.

6. Precautions and Tips

- **Do not overexert**: If your eyes feel strained or tired, stop the practice and rest your eyes. Avoid forcing your gaze for long periods, especially in the beginning.

- **Practice in a calm environment**: To enhance concentration, practice Tratak in a quiet, peaceful environment free from distractions.

- **Take care of your posture**: Sit comfortably with a straight spine to ensure the free flow of energy through the body.

- **Gradual Practice**: If you're new to Tratak, begin with a shorter duration (around 5 minutes) and gradually increase as you become more comfortable.

7. Conclusion

Tratak Kriya is an exceptional practice that not only improves concentration and mental clarity but also promotes emotional balance, eye health, and spiritual awakening. By focusing the mind and purifying the energy channels, this technique helps practitioners connect deeply with their inner selves and achieve a state of calm, peaceful awareness. Whether you are seeking to improve your focus, reduce stress, or deepen your spiritual journey, Tratak Kriya is a powerful tool to enhance your overall well-being. Through regular practice, you will find a profound transformation in your mental clarity, emotional stability, and connection with the divine.

Chapter 38:
The Meaning and Way of Reading the Bhagavad Gita

The **Bhagavad Gita** is often described as a timeless spiritual guide, offering profound wisdom and insights into life, purpose, and the nature of reality. Comprising 700 verses, this sacred text is part of the Indian epic Mahabharata and is a conversation between Lord Krishna and the warrior prince Arjuna. At its core, the Bhagavad Gita addresses the most fundamental questions of human existence: What is the purpose of life? How should one deal with challenges and dilemmas? And what is the ultimate truth?

For many years, I had heard people speak about the Bhagavad Gita and its life-changing teachings, but I never really understood its true power until I began exploring it more deeply. I started with a simple yet profound practice of reading random verses from the Gita to help me find guidance in moments of uncertainty. As I opened the pages and read the verses, I discovered a unique connection, a deep sense of clarity, and answers that I never expected. This chapter explores the significance of the Bhagavad Gita, the way to approach it, and how I started to find real solutions to my personal problems by just opening the Gita randomly and reading the chapter on the right side of the page.

The Meaning of the Bhagavad Gita

The Bhagavad Gita is not just a religious scripture; it is a philosophical and spiritual manual for living a righteous life. It transcends time, culture, and geography, offering wisdom that applies to all of humanity, regardless of religious beliefs. The Gita's teachings are universal and timeless, dealing with concepts of duty (dharma), devotion (bhakti), knowledge (jnana), and action (karma).

The conversation between Lord Krishna and Arjuna unfolds on the battlefield of Kurukshetra, where Arjuna is confused and morally troubled about fighting in the war. Arjuna faces a deep dilemma—his duty as a warrior requires him to fight, yet he is reluctant to engage in a battle that will cause pain to his loved ones. Krishna's counsel to Arjuna is filled with guidance on how to navigate the complexities of life and make decisions that align with higher spiritual principles.

The Gita teaches the **art of detachment**, the **importance of selfless action**, and the **realization of the divine presence** in all aspects of life. It explains how one can live with purpose, be free of anxiety, and face life's challenges with equanimity. Every verse contains teachings on how to be righteous, how to act without attachment to the fruits of actions, and how to seek refuge in the divine to overcome suffering and confusion.

How to Read the Bhagavad Gita

There is no single prescribed way to read the Bhagavad Gita. Different readers approach the text in different ways, depending on their spiritual journey and needs. However, there are a few important guidelines that can enhance the reading experience:

1. **Read with Intention**: Begin with a clear intention to seek knowledge, understanding, and personal growth. The Bhagavad Gita is a spiritual conversation that requires your full attention and openness. Read it with the understanding that you are connecting with the divine wisdom of Lord Krishna.

2. **One Chapter at a Time**: The Gita is divided into 18 chapters, each focusing on a specific aspect of life. Take time to read each chapter carefully and reflect on the teachings. Don't rush through the verses—let the wisdom sink in.

3. **Focus on Context**: While reading the verses, it's important to understand the context. The Gita addresses Arjuna's crisis, but its teachings go beyond the battlefield. The context can often help you apply the lessons to your own life.

4. **Meditate on the Verses**: After reading a verse or a chapter, pause and reflect. Consider how the teachings apply to your life and personal challenges. Meditation on the verses helps you internalize their meaning.

5. **Regular Practice**: Like any spiritual practice, reading the Gita regularly helps in deepening your understanding. A daily or weekly reading habit will bring clarity and peace to your life over time.

My Journey with the Bhagavad Gita

I came to the Bhagavad Gita at a time in my life when I was grappling with multiple challenges. There were moments of confusion, self-doubt, and uncertainty, and I found myself often seeking external solutions to my problems. However, one day, I remembered the practice that many people spoke about—simply opening the Bhagavad Gita randomly and reading the chapter on the right side of the page. Skeptical at first, I decided to give it a try.

I sat in a quiet space, opened the Gita, and turned the pages without any particular expectation. My eyes landed on Chapter 2, Verse 47. It spoke about performing actions without attachment to their results, and how doing one's duty without concern for the outcome brings peace of mind. This verse resonated deeply with me, as I had been constantly worrying about the results of my efforts, unable to focus purely on the action itself.

Over time, I found this practice of randomly opening the Bhagavad Gita and reading the chapter on the right side to be incredibly powerful. Every time I was stuck or confused, I would open the Gita, and the verse I landed on seemed to provide me with exactly what I needed to hear at that moment. It was as if the Gita was responding to my inner turmoil and offering solutions in real-time.

Exploring Specific Chapters of the Bhagavad Gita

As I became more familiar with the Gita, I decided to dive deeper into specific chapters that I felt held answers to some of my more pressing questions. Some of the chapters that I explored included:

1. **Chapter 2: Sankhya Yoga (The Yoga of Knowledge)**: This chapter lays the foundation for understanding the relationship between the physical world and the eternal soul (Atman). It helped me realize the importance of **detachment** from the material world and the **impermanence** of circumstances, enabling me to deal with problems more calmly.

2. **Chapter 3: Karma Yoga (The Yoga of Selfless Action)**: Here, Krishna teaches Arjuna about performing actions without attachment to the results. I found this teaching particularly liberating, as it helped me focus on the process rather than obsessing over outcomes.

3. **Chapter 4: Jnana Karma Sanyasa Yoga (The Yoga of Knowledge and Renunciation of Action)**: This chapter discusses how knowledge and action are intertwined, and the importance of acting with wisdom. It gave me a deeper understanding of how we can find purpose in even the most mundane tasks.

4. **Chapter 12: Bhakti Yoga (The Yoga of Devotion)**: As I sought deeper spiritual meaning in my life, this chapter helped me connect with the divine through **devotion**. Krishna explains that true devotion is not just about rituals but about cultivating a pure heart and living in accordance with dharma.

5. **Chapter 18: Moksha Sanyasa Yoga (The Yoga of Liberation and Renunciation)**: This final chapter provided me with clarity on the ultimate goal of life—**liberation (moksha)**. It taught me how to live a life that is in alignment with the highest truths, freeing myself from the cycle of birth and death.

Finding Solutions to Problems

What I found most remarkable about reading the Bhagavad Gita was how it provided clarity on the problems I faced in my day-to-day life. Whether it was career decisions, personal relationships, or internal conflicts, the verses of the Gita often provided unexpected solutions. It was as though the teachings directly addressed my struggles and offered guidance from a higher perspective.

For instance, whenever I felt overwhelmed with work, Chapter 2, Verse 47 reminded me to focus on my duties without getting attached to the results. When I faced doubts about my life's purpose, Chapter 3's teachings on selfless action inspired me to continue moving forward, knowing that my actions were aligned with a greater purpose.

The Bhagavad Gita, through its simple yet profound wisdom, became my spiritual compass, guiding me towards peace, clarity, and fulfillment.

Conclusion

The Bhagavad Gita is not just a text to be read—it is a guide to living a fulfilled and meaningful life. It offers solutions to problems, clarity in confusion, and a path to peace and spiritual awakening. By randomly opening the pages and reading the verses, I began to see how the Gita directly addressed my struggles and showed me a way forward. As we continue to explore its teachings, we will uncover more of its wisdom, applying it in our real lives to experience transformation, growth, and a deeper connection with the divine.

Chapter 39:
Solving Day-to-Day Life Questions Through the Bhagavad Gita

In this chapter, we explore how the Bhagavad Gita can provide practical solutions to various dilemmas we encounter in our daily lives. From stress and pressure to relationship issues and personal growth, the teachings of the Gita offer profound wisdom that can guide us to a balanced and fulfilling life. By pairing real-life questions with relevant verses from the Bhagavad Gita, we uncover timeless solutions that not only address our immediate concerns but also offer deeper insights for leading a life of peace and purpose.

1. How do I manage stress and pressure at work?

In the modern world, work-related stress is a common problem. We often feel overwhelmed with deadlines and expectations, which leads to anxiety and frustration.

Verse from Bhagavad Gita: Chapter 2, Verse 47 *"Your right is to perform your duty only, but never to its fruits. Let not the fruits of action be your motive, nor let your attachment be to inaction."*

Application:

This verse encourages us to focus on the process of work, not the outcome. When we become attached to results, stress naturally builds up. Krishna advises us to detach from the fruits of our actions, focusing only on doing our best. By adopting this approach, we reduce stress and become more present in our work.

2. How do I resolve conflicts in relationships?

Arguments and conflicts are a natural part of relationships. But they can often leave us feeling hurt, angry, or confused.

Verse from Bhagavad Gita: Chapter 16, Verse 3 *"The qualities of fearlessness, purity of heart, self-restraint, and charity are the divine qualities. Anger, pride, and selfishness belong to those with demoniacal qualities. Renounce the demoniacal qualities and develop the divine qualities to lead a peaceful life."*

Application:

Krishna advises us to cultivate qualities like fearlessness, purity, and self-restraint to overcome anger and selfishness. Instead of reacting in conflict, we should approach the situation with empathy and understanding. This helps in resolving disagreements peacefully.

3. How do I make important decisions in my life?

Life presents us with countless decisions—career choices, relationships, and more—and it's often difficult to know which path to choose.

Verse from Bhagavad Gita: Chapter 3, Verse 35 *"It is better to perform one's own duties imperfectly than to perform another's duties perfectly. It is better to die doing one's own duties; the duties of others will bring fear."*

Application:

Krishna advises us to stay true to our own path, even if it means making mistakes. Trying to imitate others only leads to fear and confusion. Trust your instincts, follow your duty, and you will find fulfillment in your decisions.

4. How can I overcome uncertainty about my life's purpose?

Many of us face periods of uncertainty, wondering what our true purpose in life is. This confusion can lead to frustration and feelings of being lost.

Verse from Bhagavad Gita: Chapter 9, Verse 22 *"To those who are constantly devoted and who remember Me with love, I give the understanding by which they can come to Me."*

Application:

This verse emphasizes the power of devotion. By dedicating ourselves to our work, relationships, and spiritual practices with love, we align ourselves with a higher purpose. This devotion naturally brings clarity about our true direction in life.

5. How do I let go of guilt and regret from the past?

Past mistakes and regrets can hold us back from moving forward. We often struggle to forgive ourselves and let go of the guilt associated with our past actions.

Verse from Bhagavad Gita: Chapter 18, Verse 66 *"Abandon all varieties of religion and just surrender unto Me. I shall deliver you from all sinful reactions; do not fear."*

Application:

Krishna encourages us to surrender our guilt and regret to Him. When we surrender, we release the weight of the past and trust in divine grace to heal us. By doing so, we free ourselves from the emotional burden that keeps us stuck in the past.

6. How can I maintain balance between work and personal life?

Finding the right balance between our professional responsibilities and personal lives can be challenging. Many times, work demands take priority, leading to neglect of personal needs and relationships.

Verse from Bhagavad Gita: Chapter 6, Verse 16 *"There is no possibility of one's becoming a yogi, O Arjuna, if one eats too much or eats too little, sleeps too much, or does not sleep enough."*

Application:

Krishna emphasizes the importance of moderation. Balancing work and personal life requires self-discipline, ensuring that neither area dominates. Maintaining a routine that includes time for work, rest, and personal relationships helps in living a balanced life.

7. Why do I feel constantly restless?

Restlessness is a common problem, often driven by an anxious mind or a sense of unfulfilled desires.

Verse from Bhagavad Gita: Chapter 6, Verse 26 *"Wherever the mind, which is restless by nature, wanders, let him subdue it and bring it under the control of the self."*

Application:

The restless mind is natural, but Krishna teaches us to control it. Meditation, mindfulness, and focusing on the present moment help in calming the mind, reducing restlessness, and increasing inner peace.

8. How can I become more patient?

Patience is a virtue, but in today's world, we often find ourselves losing our temper or becoming impatient with situations or people.

Verse from Bhagavad Gita: Chapter 16, Verse 3 *"Renounce the demoniacal qualities and develop the divine qualities to lead a peaceful life."*

Application:

By cultivating divine qualities such as patience, we develop the strength to deal with challenges calmly. Patience allows us to stay grounded, reduce anxiety, and approach life's hurdles with a clear mind.

9. How do I improve my focus and concentration?

Distractions and a wandering mind can hinder our ability to focus and concentrate, especially in today's technology-driven world.

Verse from Bhagavad Gita: Chapter 6, Verse 5 *"One must elevate, not degrade, oneself with one's own mind. The mind is the friend of the conditioned soul, and his enemy as well."*

Application:

Krishna tells us that the mind can either be our greatest ally or our worst enemy. To improve concentration, we must train the mind through practice and discipline. Meditation and focused attention are ways to strengthen the mind and increase our ability to concentrate.

10. How do I deal with fear and anxiety?

Fear and anxiety often hold us back from taking action and stepping into new opportunities.

Verse from Bhagavad Gita: Chapter 2, Verse 13 *"Just as the boyhood, youth and old age come to the embodied Soul in this body, in the same manner, old age comes to the soul; and the soul is never born, nor does it die."*

Application:

Krishna assures us that the soul is eternal and indestructible. Understanding this truth helps us overcome the fear of change, death, and the unknown. When we recognize that we are not our fears, we can approach life with courage and calm.

11. How can I stay motivated when I feel uninspired?

Sometimes we lose motivation, especially when the tasks at hand feel monotonous or overwhelming.

Verse from Bhagavad Gita: Chapter 2, Verse 47 *"Perform your duties with concentration and devotion, without being attached to the results."*

Application:

This verse teaches us that our motivation should come from a sense of duty and devotion to the work itself. By focusing on the action rather than the outcome, we can reignite our passion and stay motivated even during difficult times.

12. Why do I feel disconnected from my spirituality?

Spiritual disconnection can occur when life becomes too busy or when we face doubts about our faith or practices.

Verse from Bhagavad Gita: Chapter 9, Verse 22 *"To those who are constantly devoted and who remember Me with love, I give the understanding by which they can come to Me."*

Application:

Through devotion, we reconnect with our spirituality. Krishna assures that when we remember Him with love and sincerity, our spiritual understanding deepens. Devotional practices such as prayer and meditation can help restore this connection.

13. How do I forgive others who have wronged me?

Forgiving those who have hurt us can be one of the most challenging emotional tasks.

Verse from Bhagavad Gita: Chapter 16, Verse 3 *"Renounce the demoniacal qualities and develop the divine qualities to lead a peaceful life."*

Application:

Forgiveness is a divine quality. Krishna teaches us to let go of anger and resentment and instead cultivate compassion and understanding. Forgiving others frees us from emotional burdens and allows us to heal.

14. How do I balance my personal desires with my responsibilities?

We often struggle to fulfill personal desires while fulfilling societal or familial duties, creating inner conflict.

Verse from Bhagavad Gita: Chapter 3, Verse 35 *"It is better to perform one's own duties imperfectly than to perform another's duties perfectly."*

Application:

This verse advises us to stay true to our own responsibilities. By fulfilling our personal duties with dedication, we find contentment and fulfillment. Trying to satisfy others at the expense of our own desires leads to dissatisfaction.

15. How can I make peace with failure?

Failure can be a bitter experience, often leading to self-doubt and discouragement.

Verse from Bhagavad Gita: Chapter 2, Verse 14 *"O son of Kunti, the nonpermanent appearance of happiness and distress, and their disappearance in due course, are like the appearance and disappearance of winter and summer seasons. They arise from sense perception, and one must learn to tolerate them without being disturbed."*

Application:

Krishna reminds us that both happiness and distress are temporary. By viewing failure as part of a larger cycle of life and understanding that challenges are opportunities for growth, we can face them with resilience and peace.

16. How do I deal with feelings of jealousy and comparison?

Jealousy and comparison often arise when we measure ourselves against others' success or possessions.

Verse from Bhagavad Gita: Chapter 12, Verse 13-14 *"One who is not envious but is a kind friend to all, who is free from possessiveness, and who is unaffected by success or failure, is a true devotee of God."*

Application:

Krishna teaches us to be content with who we are and focus on self-improvement. Instead of comparing ourselves to others, we should celebrate our uniqueness and be non-envious of others' successes. This helps in cultivating inner peace.

17. How can I develop self-discipline in my life?

Lack of discipline often hinders personal growth and achievement, leading to procrastination and missed opportunities.

Verse from Bhagavad Gita: Chapter 6, Verse 5 *"One must elevate, not degrade, oneself with one's own mind. The mind is the friend of the conditioned soul, and his enemy as well."*

Application:

Krishna emphasizes the importance of self-control. Discipline begins with mastering the mind. To develop self-discipline, we must establish routines, set clear goals, and focus on our actions. The mind must be trained to work towards positive objectives.

18. How can I stay calm in difficult situations?

Difficult situations often trigger panic, fear, or anxiety, making it harder to think clearly or act wisely.

Verse from Bhagavad Gita: Chapter 2, Verse 14 *"O son of Kunti, the nonpermanent appearance of happiness and distress, and their disappearance in due course, are like the appearance and disappearance of winter and summer seasons. They arise from sense perception, and one must learn to tolerate them without being disturbed."*

Application:

Krishna advises us to tolerate the ups and downs of life, understanding that they are temporary. By recognizing the impermanence of challenges, we can maintain a calm and composed demeanor, even in difficult times.

19. How do I stop overthinking and enjoy the present?

Overthinking can trap us in cycles of worry and indecision, preventing us from living in the moment.

Verse from Bhagavad Gita: Chapter 3, Verse 16 *"One who does not follow the wheel of creation set of God, sinful and sensual; he lives in vain."*

Application:

Krishna encourages us to focus on the present moment and the duties at hand. By engaging fully in the task at hand, rather than overthinking future outcomes, we can break the cycle of anxiety and be more mindful.

20. How can I be more compassionate and understanding toward others?

In a world that often feels competitive and harsh, showing compassion can help build better relationships.

Verse from Bhagavad Gita: Chapter 12, Verse 13-14 *"One who is free from malice, who has no hatred for anyone, who is content, who has control over his senses, and who is unaffected by praise or blame is dear to Me."*

Application:

Krishna highlights the importance of being kind and free from malice. To develop compassion, we must practice tolerance, avoid judgment, and develop a deeper understanding of others' situations and struggles.

21. How do I handle failure without losing confidence?

Failure often brings feelings of self-doubt and can make us question our capabilities.

Verse from Bhagavad Gita: Chapter 2, Verse 47 *"Your right is to perform your duty only, but never to its fruits. Let not the fruits of action be your motive, nor let your attachment be to inaction."*

Application:

Krishna teaches us to detach from the results of our efforts. Focusing solely on doing our best, regardless of the outcome, helps in accepting failure as a part of the learning process. This builds resilience and strengthens confidence.

22. How can I stop feeling overwhelmed by life's responsibilities?

The weight of responsibilities can often feel burdensome, especially when we have too many obligations.

Verse from Bhagavad Gita: Chapter 18, Verse 66 *"Abandon all varieties of religion and just surrender unto Me. I shall deliver you from all sinful reactions; do not fear."*

Application:

Krishna assures us that surrendering our worries to Him and trusting the process can bring relief. By letting go of the need to control everything, we invite peace and clarity. This helps in managing responsibilities with a lighter heart.

23. How do I stay grounded and humble in success?

Success can sometimes lead to arrogance and ego, making us lose sight of humility and gratitude.

Verse from Bhagavad Gita: Chapter 13, Verse 8-12 *"Humility, non-violence, patience, simplicity, self-control, and compassion are the divine qualities."*

Application:

Krishna highlights that humility is essential for spiritual growth. To stay grounded in success, we must remember that all accomplishments are a result of divine blessings and collective effort. Acknowledging others' contributions keeps us humble.

24. How can I deal with the fear of the unknown?

The fear of uncertainty about the future can often paralyze us, preventing us from taking action.

Verse from Bhagavad Gita: Chapter 9, Verse 22 *"To those who are constantly devoted and who remember Me with love, I give the understanding by which they can come to Me."*

Application:

Krishna assures that by dedicating ourselves to Him with love and devotion, we gain clarity and understanding. This divine guidance helps us navigate uncertain situations with confidence, knowing that the future is in good hands.

25. How do I handle the feeling of not being good enough?

Many people struggle with feelings of inadequacy and the fear that they aren't living up to their potential.

Verse from Bhagavad Gita: Chapter 2, Verse 40 *"In this endeavor, there is no loss or diminution, and a little advancement on this path can protect one from the most dangerous type of fear."*

Application:

Krishna reassures us that any effort on the spiritual or self-improvement path is never wasted. Even small progress in our journey counts and brings us closer to our goals. We should never feel inadequate because every step forward matters.

26. How can I stop being so hard on myself?

Often, we are our harshest critics, leading to self-doubt, guilt, and burnout.

Verse from Bhagavad Gita: Chapter 6, Verse 30 *"One who sees Me in all beings, and all beings in Me, is never separated from Me, and I am never separated from him."*

Application:

Krishna teaches us to see the divine in ourselves and others. When we recognize that we are part of a larger whole, we begin to treat ourselves with more kindness and compassion. Self-forgiveness becomes easier, and we let go of unrealistic expectations.

27. How do I manage the fear of failure in my career?

The fear of failure often holds us back from pursuing our dreams or taking necessary risks in our careers.

Verse from Bhagavad Gita: Chapter 18, Verse 63 *"Thus, I have explained to you this knowledge that is more secret than all secrets. Ponder over it deeply, and then do as you wish."*

Application:

Krishna reminds us that fear is a part of life. We must approach our career with the understanding that failure is an opportunity for growth. By contemplating our choices, we find the courage to move forward, trusting that all experiences, whether good or bad, offer valuable lessons.

28. How can I build better self-esteem?

Self-esteem is often impacted by external validation, and we may struggle when we don't receive it.

Verse from Bhagavad Gita: Chapter 2, Verse 50 *"A person who is unaffected by pleasure and pain, who is free from doubt and fear, is truly wise."*

Application:

Krishna advises us to not depend on external validation. By learning to regulate our own reactions to life's circumstances and remaining unaffected by praise or criticism, we can cultivate true self-esteem from within.

29. How do I deal with guilt from past mistakes?

Guilt from past mistakes can weigh heavily on our minds, preventing us from moving forward in life.

Verse from Bhagavad Gita: Chapter 9, Verse 30 *"Even if a person of the most sinful nature worships Me with undivided devotion, he is to be considered righteous, for he has rightly resolved."*

Application:

Krishna assures us that no matter what wrongs we may have committed, sincere devotion and self-realization can purify us. Guilt arises when we are unable to forgive ourselves, but through genuine effort and commitment to change, we can move forward without being burdened by past mistakes.

30. How can I find a deeper sense of purpose in life?

Sometimes, we struggle with finding a deeper sense of purpose, which leads to feelings of emptiness or confusion.

Verse from Bhagavad Gita: Chapter 3, Verse 35 *"Performing one's own duties, even if imperfectly, is better than performing another's duties perfectly. It is better to die fulfilling one's own duties than to live performing another's duties."*

Application:

Krishna teaches that true fulfillment comes from performing the duties that align with our nature and purpose. When we pursue the tasks that resonate with our inner values and passions, we discover a deeper meaning in life. By focusing on our unique path, we find purpose and satisfaction in the present moment.

CONCLUSION:

The Bhagavad Gita offers practical solutions for every aspect of our daily lives, addressing issues such as stress, decision-making, conflict resolution, and personal growth. By integrating the teachings of the Gita into our lives, we can navigate life's challenges with wisdom, clarity, and peace.

Chapter 40:
Guru Diksha

Guru Diksha, or the initiation given by a Guru, holds an esteemed place in the spiritual traditions of India. It is the process through which a disciple receives spiritual guidance, teachings, and blessings from a Guru (spiritual master). Guru Diksha is not just a ritualistic practice, but an essential step in one's spiritual evolution. This chapter will explore the significance of Guru Diksha, its rituals, and the profound impact it has on an individual's life.

The Meaning of Guru Diksha

The word "Diksha" is derived from the Sanskrit word "Dik" meaning direction and "Sha" meaning to give. So, Guru Diksha refers to the initiation or blessing from the Guru, providing the disciple with guidance, wisdom, and spiritual discipline. The Guru acts as the guiding light, helping the disciple on their spiritual journey, and Diksha is a formal process of entering the sacred bond of disciple and teacher.

The Ritual of Guru Diksha

The ceremony of Guru Diksha is simple but profound. It usually involves the disciple bowing down before the Guru, offering prayers and gratitude, and receiving a sacred mantra or teaching. The Guru may give the disciple a specific spiritual practice, mantra, or a set of rules to follow for spiritual growth. The Guru Diksha ceremony may also involve the use of sacred items like water, flowers, or fire.

The process symbolizes the transfer of divine wisdom from the Guru to the disciple. This initiation can happen at a particular time, such as during an auspicious festival or on the birth anniversary of a revered Guru. The ceremony may take place in temples, ashrams, or at the Guru's residence.

Significance of Guru Diksha

1. **Transformation**: Guru Diksha marks the beginning of a new phase in a disciple's life. It transforms their perception, leading them onto the path of wisdom, self-realization, and spiritual awakening.

2. **Discipline and Devotion**: By accepting Diksha, the disciple commits to following the teachings of the Guru. It instills a sense of discipline, devotion, and humility.

3. **Spiritual Guidance**: The Guru provides the disciple with the right path, removing confusion and guiding them toward higher spiritual knowledge. Diksha ensures that the disciple has the proper tools to pursue this path.

4. **Sacred Connection**: Guru Diksha is a sacred bond between the disciple and the Guru. It establishes a lifelong connection that transcends time and space. The blessings received during Diksha carry immense significance throughout the disciple's spiritual journey.

5. **Overcoming Obstacles**: The Guru's blessings empower the disciple to face life's challenges with strength and resilience. Guru Diksha provides the disciple with divine protection and support.

6. **Inner Peace and Bliss**: The mantra or teachings given during Diksha help the disciple attain inner peace and harmony. Over time, this practice leads to a blissful state of mind and spiritual fulfillment.

The Role of a Guru

The Guru plays a pivotal role in the initiation process. The Guru is not only a teacher but a spiritual guide, a mentor, and a protector. The Guru must possess qualities of wisdom, compassion, and humility. Through their teachings, the Guru helps the disciple transcend the limitations of the physical world and realize their divine nature.

Guru Diksha is not just about receiving teachings; it is about developing a deep relationship with the Guru, who walks with the disciple every step of the way, helping them navigate the spiritual journey.

Impact of Guru Diksha on Daily Life

Once the disciple receives Guru Diksha, their life takes on a new meaning. They begin to see the world with a more awakened perspective. Their thoughts become more aligned with the higher purpose, and they start living with a greater sense of responsibility, humility, and wisdom. The practices and teachings given during Diksha guide them in their daily life, transforming mundane tasks into acts of devotion.

Guru Diksha and Its Relevance in Modern Times

In today's fast-paced world, Guru Diksha continues to hold immense significance. Even as materialism and distractions take over, the need for spiritual guidance is as strong as ever. Guru Diksha helps individuals find inner peace amidst the chaos and connect to their deeper selves. It serves as a reminder that we are not just physical beings, but spiritual beings on a journey toward enlightenment.

Many spiritual traditions today still emphasize the importance of Guru Diksha. Whether through formal ceremonies or informal teachings, the bond between Guru and disciple remains a sacred and invaluable part of one's spiritual life.

Conclusion

Guru Diksha is a powerful and transformative process that connects the disciple with the eternal wisdom and guidance of the Guru. It is a vital practice for anyone on a spiritual path, offering support, clarity, and protection. The teachings and practices imparted during Diksha illuminate the path of the disciple, leading them toward self-realization and inner peace.

As we walk through life, the blessings of Guru Diksha remain with us, shaping our thoughts, actions, and spiritual progress.

Chapter 41:
Do Haircuts According to Moon Phase Help in Hair Growth

What's the idea behind lunar haircare?

Whether it's the **lunar hair cutting chart** or cosmic rituals, the idea behind moon guidance is strong. A strong inclination towards lunar haircare stems from the belief that it can help you get longer, thicker, and more lustrous hair. It simply involves syncing hair trims or cuts with the lunar cycles. Stefani Padilla, hairstylist and shaman to MBG, said, "The pull of the full moon and new moon creates a healthier, more productive garden. This is the same approach we take in lunar haircare".

During moon phases, the gravitational pull influences the high and low ocean tides, causing the rise of moisture on Earth. Our bodies are mostly made of water, which also impacts our thoughts. Even if it is not noticeable, lunar and hair growth cycles are in sync. The extra moisture in the environment around the new moon makes your hair feel good and healthy. While the majority is astrological, some science is associated with lunar haircare.

Lunar Haircutting Sees an Upward Trend

There is a strong belief that the moon affects hair in many ways. Many people are guided by the lunar cycle when contemplating coloring or cutting their hair. The concept of a new moon haircut is rooted in spiritual awareness—it is a ceremonial representation of letting go of the old and embracing the new. **Lunar hair-cutting charts**, as per hairstrology, harness the moon's magic to bring a refreshing change to the locks.

Moon-inspired haircuts have increased with people scheduling styling, trims, or cuts around the New Moon. The concept of lunar haircutting is rooted in spirituality and brings a deep appreciation. People have claimed to feel good and positive energy around them with trims or haircuts synced around the New Moon. TikTok has raked 1.2 billion views on the hashtag #newmoonhaircut, which interests the masses.

Moon Phases for Lunar Hair Cutting Charts

The lunar haircare charts vary every month as the lunar cycle changes. Also, the dates vary from the Northern to the Southern hemisphere. Each month, the days favorable for a haircut, trim, or opting for a change varies. The 28-day lunar cycle begins with a new moon. However, the phases of the moon remain the same. Let's understand each moon phase and how to sync it with haircare.

New Moon – Setting New Hair Goals

From an astrological perspective, the new moon is ideal for setting goals as it is the beginning of the lunar cycle. It marks the onset of the lunar cycle, where seeds of intention are sprinkled, and full bloom is manifested. As per the lunar haircare narrative, it's that time to set affirmations for the growth of beautiful, healthy, and luscious locks. Avoid cutting your hair during the new moon, but extend care through deep conditioning treatments and a good routine.

Waxing Moon – Manifesting Hair Growth

As the new moon transitions to complete, it is met by the waxing moon phase in between. This makes this transition lunar phase perfect for trims and eliminating dead ends. By letting go of the unwanted, it is time for hair regeneration. As believed by hairstrology, the waxing crescent moon boosts hair growth and restores and repairs damage. Team up the trims with nourishing treatments like a hair spa or a hydrating hair mask.

Full Moon – Cut, Treat, and Color

It is considered one of the most powerful lunar phases, focusing on intensifying transition and bringing changes. It's when the moon is most visible and symbolic of releasing old burdens. This is a perfect time to get a haircut, remove damaged hair, and make way for thick and healthy growth. As new moons are also favorable for new beginnings, try a new hair color or treatment to change your hairstyle positively.

Waning Moon – Slow down of growth

This brings us to the end of the lunar cycle, representing ends linked to new beginnings. After the complete moon phase, this phase indicates decelerated hair growth. If you want to keep your hair short, this might be the best time. You can opt for a trim or cut off the damaged ends to maintain healthy hair for longer.

Intersection of Science and Spirituality

Moehair has got to the bottom of it to understand if there is an actual connection between **lunar hair cutting charts** and the well-being of hair. Scientifically, there is no proven link between lunar haircare and hair growth. However, the belief stems from manifesting positivity and consciously putting in efforts to care for hair. Lunar haircutting is not scientifically backed, but it's worth trying as it encourages ritualistic care and positive affirmations. To conclude, following haircare rituals like trimming, cutting, treatment, or coloring based on moon phases shifts focus on dedicated haircare every month.

Chapter 42:
Pradakshina: Why Do We Go Clockwise Around Temples

Pradakshina means circumambulation. Circumambulation means going in a clockwise direction, particularly in the northern hemisphere. In the northern hemisphere of the planet, this is a natural phenomenon. If you notice closely, many natural phenomenon turn clockwise above the Equator and anticlockwise below it. It is not just with air or water, the very energy system functions like this.

This is why if there is an energetic place in the northern hemisphere, and you want to derive benefit from or absorb the energy, you must go clockwise around it. If you want to benefit more, your hair should be wet. If you want to benefit even more, your clothes should also be wet. If you want to benefit still more, you must go around naked. But wet clothes are probably better than nakedness because the body dries up very soon. Clothes remain wet for a long time. So wet clothes are the best way to go around any energy space because you will receive it best – you are most receptive that way.

This is why every temple had a water body what was generally called a *kalyani*. In Tamil Nadu, it is called a *kulam*. You are supposed to take a dip and go through the temple with wet clothes so that you receive the energies of the consecrated space in the best possible way. But today, most of the kulams have either gone dry or mostly gone filthy.

窗体底端

A Vortex of Energies

When you go clockwise, you are moving with certain natural forces. Any consecrated space functions like a vortex which means that it reverberates, and it also draws. Both ways, an intermingling of what we are referring to as the divine and what we are calling as the self, happens. The idea in this culture is that we don't want to meet God, we don't want to go to heaven and sit on his lap. Here, we want to become God – we are very ambitious people. We are not looking at seeing the divine. We want to realize and become divine. The idea of being in a consecrated space is to constantly allow this transaction to happen, so that gradually, the living body itself becomes like a divine entity. If you want, you can keep this body like a beast. Or you can make it like a sacred form or divinity.

Going clockwise around a consecrated space is a simple way of receiving this possibility. Particularly from the equator up to thirty-three degrees latitude, this is very intense. That is why we set up most temples within this region because this is where you get maximum benefit. You can clearly see that as you go up north, temples were set up mainly for devotion. In the south, the devotion aspect is there but the most important thing is they are scientifically constructed in a certain way – magnificent structures which took lifetimes to create.

A Different Kind of Humanity

Many temples took many generations of people to build. For example, the Kailash temple at Ellora, which was built by the Rashtrakutas took 135 years of work. That means four generations of people worked to the same plan, not changing a bit. That takes a different kind of humanity. Today, the whole of humanity has become such that, anything you give them, they want to do one silly innovation. It does not matter how silly it is, they want to leave their footprint on everything. Such magnificent temples were built, but no one left a name or initial anywhere to say, "I did it." They simply worked and died without completing it. The next generation took it on, worked and died without completing it. The next generation came along, they worked and they died. They knew that someone is going to complete it.

This is a different kind of humanity. We want to produce those kind of people because those are the people who will do things which are truly worthwhile for humanity. We want to produce that kind of humanity who are god-like. When I say god-like, this is such a magnificent creation, but did the Creator leave His signature somewhere? No. He stands back to such an extent that we can sit here and debate whether there is a Creator or not.

Chapter 43:
What Happens If You Don't Eat for a Full Day?
(24-hour fast)

- Is it safe?
- Effects on body
- Benefits
- Potential side effects and risks
- Water intake
- How to
- Bottom line

Intermittent fasting can involve going a full day without eating. It may help your body use stored fat for energy, but there may be risks involved.

Not eating for 24 hours at a time is a form of intermittent fasting known as the eat-stop-eat approach.

During a 24-hour fast, you can only consume calorie-free beverages. When the 24-hour period is over, you can resume your typical intake of food until the next fast.

This practice may not be safe for everyone. It's important to speak with a doctor about whether it will be safe for you to do so before fasting.

Learn more about what happens to your body if you don't eat for a full day, the benefits, and whether it is safe.

Is it a safe practice?

In addition to weight loss, intermittent fasting may positively affect metabolism, boost cardiovascular health, and more. It's typically safe to use this approach once or twice a week to achieve your desired results.

Although this technique may seem easier than cutting back on daily calories, you may find yourself quite "hangry" on fasting days. It can also cause severe side effects or complications in people with certain health conditions.

You should always talk with a doctor before going on a fast. They can advise you on your individual benefits and risks. Keep reading to learn more.

ADVERTISEMENT

What happens to your body during this time

You'll be well into your 24-hour period before your body realizes that you're fasting.

During the first 6 hours, your body will continue to digest your last intake of food. Your body will use stored glucose, called glycogen, as energy and continue to function as though you'll be eating again soon.

After several hours without eating, your body will begin to use stored fats for energy throughout the remainder of your 24-hour fast.

Fasts that last longer than 24 hours may lead your body to start converting stored proteins into energy.

Are there benefits to this approach?

More research is needed to fully understand how intermittent fasting can affect your body. Early research does suggest a few benefits, though.

Help with weight loss

Fasting 1 or 2 days a week mayTrusted Source be a way to consume fewer calories over time. You may find this easier than cutting back a certain number of calories every day. The energy restriction from a 24-hour fast may also benefit your metabolism, helping in weight loss.

Manage cholesterol and sugar levels

Regular intermittent fasting may help improve how your body breaks down cholesterol and sugar. These changes to your metabolism may help reduce your risk of developing conditions like diabetes and cardiovascular disease.

Reduce risk for coronary artery disease

A regular 24-hour fast may help reduce trimethylamine N-oxide levels in the long term. High levels of this compound are tied to coronary artery disease, so this may help reduce your risk.

Are there side effects or risks to doing this?

Frequently fasting for 24 hours at a time can lead to side effects and increase your risk for certain complications.

Always talk with a doctor before going on a fast to help reduce your risk for any unforeseen health consequences. This is particularly important if you have underlying health conditions.

You shouldn't fast if you:

- have or have had an eating disorder
- have type 1 diabetes
- are pregnant or breastfeeding or chestfeeding
- are under the age of 18
- are recovering from surgery

Fasting more than twice per week may increase your risk for heart arrhythmias and hypoglycemia.

Keep in mind that more research is needed to fully assess the potential benefits and risks of intermittent fasting. Exercising regularly and eating a balanced diet are proven methods for living a healthier lifestyle and maintaining your weight.

Will drinking water during the fast help?

During a 24-hour fast, it's important to drink plenty of water—more than your usual 8 glasses.

You won't be ingesting any water from food during this time, and your body needs water to function. Water helps your digestive system regulate your body temperature benefits your joints and tissues, and can keep you feeling energized.

You should drink water as you feel thirsty throughout the day. The amount you should drink varies from person to person and depends on your activity level.

How to eat-stop-eat the right way

You can perform a 24-hour fast whenever you choose. You just have to make sure that you prepare for your fasting day in advance. Eating healthy and well-rounded meals prior to the fast will help your body get through the 24-hour period.

Some foods you should consider eating prior to fast include:

- foods rich in protein, such as nut butter and beans
- dairy products low in fat, such as low fat yogurt
- fruits and vegetables
- Whole grain starches

Foods high in fiber can help your body feel full long after eating. Fruits and vegetables contain water, giving you more hydration.

Keep in mind that beverages with caffeine may cause you to lose more water. Drink an additional cup of water for every caffeinated beverage to help balance your intake.

You may want to have a small snack or eat a light meal when your fast ends to help you ease back into your regular eating routine.

The bottom line

It is important to be cautious when trying this approach. Talk with a doctor about your health before attempting it on your own. They can help you understand individual benefits and risks, as well as advise you on how to conduct this type of fast in a healthy and safe way.

Chapter 44:
Kumbh Mela, Explained: Its Mythology, History, Astrology, and Why Millions Flock to It

Maha Kumbh Mela Mythology, History, Astrology: It is cold in Prayagraj, foggy with a chance of rain. Yet, on Monday (January 13), tens of thousands are expected to arrive in the city, to camp on the banks of the Ganga. They will stay in tents and bathe in the river, the most devout taking a dip at dawn while stars are still twinkling.

Prayagraj is hosting the Maha Kumbh this time, or the **Poorna Kumbh, held every 12 years**. Many myths are prevalent around the Kumbh Mela, many theories about its exact origin. Some believe the festival finds mention in the Vedas and Puranas. Some say it is far more recent, going back barely two centuries. What is known for certain is that today, it is one of the largest gatherings of devotees witnessed anywhere on earth.

What is the Kumbh Mela, and why is it held in four cities periodically? What is Ardh Kumbh and Maha Kumbh? What is the origin of this festival, and why do millions attend it?

The answers, as in many questions about Hinduism, lie in a mixture of myths, history, and the enduring faith of an ancient people, trusting as much in the munificence of invisible deities as in tangible life-givers like rivers.

The mythological origins of the Kumbh Mela

The Sanskrit word *kumbh* means pitcher, or pot. The story goes that when Devas (gods) and Asuras (loosely translated as demons) churned the ocean, Dhanvantri emerged carrying a pitcher of *amrita*, or the elixir of immortality. To make sure the Asuras don't get it, Indra's son, Jayant, ran off with the pot. The

Sun, his son Shani, Brihaspati (the planet Jupiter), and the Moon went along to protect him and the pot.

As Jayant ran, the *amrita* spilt at four spots: Haridwar, Prayagraj, Ujjain, and Nashik-Trimbakeshwar. He ran for 12 days, and as one day of the Devas is equal to one year of humans, Kumbh Mela is celebrated at these locations every 12 years, based on the relative positions of the Sun, the Moon, and Jupiter.

Prayagraj and Haridwar also hold the Ardh-Kumbh (*ardh* means half), every six years. The festival held after 12 years is called the Poorna Kumbh, or the Maha Kumbh.

All four places are located on the banks of rivers — Haridwar has the Ganga, Prayagraj is the sangam or meeting point of Ganga, Yamuna and the mythical Saraswati, Ujjain has the Kshipra, and Nashik-Trimbakeshwar the Godavari.

It is believed that taking a dip in these rivers during Kumbh, amid the specific alignment of the heavenly bodies, washes away one's sins and accrues punya (spiritual merit).

Kumbh Melas are also the venue where Sadhus and other holy men gather — the *sadhu akhadaas* attracting a lot of curiosity — and regular people can meet them and learn from them.

"While the importance of the Ganga in Hindu religion is well-known, the Kshipra is believed to have emerged from the heart of Vishnu in his *Varah* (boar) avatar. The Godavari is often called the Ganga of Dakshin (south)," Dr Dipakbhai Jyotishacharya, who runs the Parashar Jyotishalaya in Gujarat's Vapi, told The Indian Express.

How is the site of a Kumbh Mela decided?

This depends on astrological calculations. Another reason for the 12-year gap in Kumbh Melas is explained by the fact that Jupiter takes 12 years to complete on revolution around the Sun.

According to the Kumbh Mela website, when Jupiter is in Aquarius or Kumbh *rashi* (whose symbol is the water bearer), and

Sun and Moon in <u>Aries</u> and <u>Sagittarius</u> respectively, Kumbh is held at Haridwar.

When the Jupiter is in <u>Taurus</u>, and the Sun and Moon are in <u>Capricorn</u> or Makar (thus, Makar Sankranti is also in this period) the Kumbh is held at Prayag.

When Jupiter is in <u>Leo</u> or Simha, and the Sun and Moon in <u>Cancer</u>, the Kumbh is held at Nashik and Trimbakeshwar, which is why they are also called the Simhastha Kumbh.

Chapter 45:
Rangoli, A Colourful Science of Symmetry

Rangoli-making is a serious business in my locality. Each morning, swish-swoosh go the brooms as front yards are swept and washed clean. Then come out the small bowls of white powder, and within minutes, women adeptly lay beautiful patterns on the fl...

Sometimes red brick powder accompanies the white, enhancing the graphic effect. However, it is during the festive season that the best art is on display: elaborate patterns encompassing designs of flowers, vines, motifs, and images of deities are laiid out. Plain white or coloured, they are a visual treat, leaving me in awe.

Humans have communicated through symbols since ancient times. Symbolism exists in every culture and takes precedence at ceremonies; reportedly, some native African groups lay specific patterns to attract animals for hunting. Rangolis are symbolic representations too, prevalent as an art form in India, and a few other Asian countries. Known by different names, they have roots in the Sanskrit word 'rangavalli' (colourful vines). With spiritual and cultural significance attached to them, festivals are incomplete without rangolis.

Our culture assigns an essential status to rangolis as they are believed to ward off evils, bring peace and prosperity to the dwelling. Specific designs chosen for prayer areas are said to radiate positive energy. However, there is more to rangolis than meets the eye. It's all science!

While rangolis occupy the artistic platform, one cannot but be surprised to realise that there is incredible science hidden behind it. This daily ritualistic practice in many parts of India incorporates a profound understanding of neuroscience.

A striking aspect of an orthodox rangoli is dots — specifically 108 — joined by curved lines to form a symmetrical design. From an artistic point of view, symmetry represents order, harmony and serenity. Symmetry is an innate quality of nature seen from the single-celled to complex organisms. This stable form of visual property — called visual harmonic — is well perceived by our brain, and we respond to it immediately.

It was Ernst Mach who first studied human response to symmetry. His research also revealed that humans are more sensitive to vertical symmetry. Further studies in 2002 observed that our brain is wired to perceive symmetry either consciously or unconsciously and forms a universal element in all that we construct — art to architecture.

Just as symmetrical notes induce a pleasing effect on the mind, responding to visual harmonic has a calming effect on the brain. Neuroscience addresses Cymatics with interest as it has a soothing effect on the mind. Some studies indicate therapeutic qualities to it. Another research shows that rapid, efficient perceptual processing of symmetrical objects produces a happy hedonic feeling.

Profound wisdom: Rangolis are geometrically balanced optical waveforms and drawing them is no simple task. To reproduce a symmetrical pattern, one must actively use both the right and the left part of the brain, simultaneously running the coarse powder through the fingers, which together activate nerve centres in the brain.

This intricate art has been mentioned in the epics of Ramayana and Mahabharata, wherein the people drew rangavallis to welcome their kings and express their joy. This amalgam of science and tradition reflects the profound and deep scientific knowledge our ancestors possessed. What they found was made available to the larger populace through simple traditions and rituals to benefit from — as an art form to be practised.

So why not let every festive season inspire us to try our hand at drawing some traditional rangolis? As we know, this indulgence has plenty on offer and could be just what the doctor ordered to counteract the perils of a hectic lifestyle!

Conclusion

As we reach the end of "Drama Decoded: Tradition Meets Science," we reflect on the profound connection between the ancient traditions that have been passed down through generations and the modern scientific understanding that continues to evolve. This journey through cultural practices, rituals, and customs has opened a new perspective, revealing that what might initially seem like mere superstition or blind adherence to tradition often carries with it deeper significance — a balance of spiritual, mental, and physical well-being.

From the symbolism behind everyday practices like wearing a toe ring or the science of chanting mantras to the deeper understanding of rituals such as Surya Namaskar and the science behind our connection with nature, this book has provided insight into how our ancestors integrated knowledge of the body, mind, and the environment into their customs. These practices were never arbitrary; instead, they were grounded in ancient wisdom that aligns closely with scientific principles, even before they were formally recognized by modern science.

The book also aimed to challenge preconceived notions and shed light on the hidden powers within these traditions. It encouraged us to question, understand, and ultimately appreciate the practices that are often part of our daily lives. Through reflection, we have gained clarity on how each act, whether simple or complex, serves a higher purpose, ensuring holistic growth.

As we conclude, we are reminded that the union of tradition and science is not an abstract concept but a tangible reality in our lives. We are encouraged to embrace both: to value the time-tested wisdom passed down through our ancestors, while also seeking knowledge through the lens of science. The combination of the two opens doors to a deeper understanding of ourselves and the world around us.

May this book inspire you to explore these traditions with new eyes and unlock the hidden science behind every gesture, thought, and practice. In doing so, may you find harmony, health, and a deeper connection to the universe around you, as we continue to decode the drama that unfolds in our everyday lives.